CLERKS

CLERKS

Kevin Smith

faber and faber

CLERKS

Kevin Smith

faber and faber

First published in the United States in 1997
by Miramax/Hyperion

Published by arrangement with Hyperion,
114 Fifth Avenue, New York, New York 10011, USA

First published in the United Kingdom in 1997
by Faber and Faber Limited
3 Queen Square London WC1N 3AU

This edition published in 2000

Printed in Great Britain by Mackays of Chatham plc,
Chatham, Kent

A CIP record for this book
is available from the British Library

ISBN 0-571-20229-2

2 4 6 8 10 9 7 5 3 1

For Joey—who sat through many new ''theories'' and talked me though countless processing complications with wonderful patience, suffered me like a child, maintained her honor and dignity in the face of my insecure accusations, and continues to help me understand the simple lesson that comprehension of the past, not condemnation, is the only manner in which to neutralize insecurity . . . and all while still making *me* feel like the smart one.

CLERKS

INT: BEDROOM. EARLY-MORNING HOURS

A DOG *sleeps on a neatly made bed.*
A CLOCK *reads twenty to six.*
A SHELF OF BOOKS *holds such classics as* Dante's Inferno, Beyond
Good and Evil, The Catcher in the Rye, *and* The Dark Knight Returns. A
FRAMED DIPLOMA, *dusty and unkempt, hangs askew on the wall. A
snapshot of a girl is stuck in the corner, and a bra weighs one end down.
A* PHONE *sits quietly atop a bundle of laundry. It suddenly explodes with
a resounding ring—once, twice, three times. A* CLOSET DOOR *swings
open, and a half-clad figure falls out.* THE PHONE *rings yet again, and
a hand falls upon the receiver, yanking it off the trash can, OC.* THE
RUMPLED FIGURE *lays with his back to the camera, phone in hand.*

> FIGURE
> *(groggily)*
> Hello . . . What? . . . No, I don't work today. . . . I'm playing
> hockey at two.

THE DOG *yawns and shakes its head.*

> FIGURE (OC)
> Why don't you call Randal? . . . Because I'm fucking tired. . . . I
> just closed last night. . . .
> *(deep sigh)*
> Jesus . . . What time are you going to come in? . . . Twelve . . . Be
> there by twelve? . . . Swear . . .

A PICTURE OF A GIRL *leans against a trophy. The picture is decorated
with a Play-Doh beard and mustache.*

FIGURE (OC)
Swear you'll be in by twelve and I'll do it. . . .
Twelve . . . Twelve or I walk.

THE PHONE RECEIVER *slams into the cradle.* THE RUMPLED
FIGURE *slowly sits up and remains motionless. He musses his hair and
stands.*
THE DOG *stands and wags its tail. A hand pats its head. The Rumpled
Figure lays down on the bed. We now see his face. It is the face of* DANTE
and this is Dante's room; this is Dante's life. DANTE *grabs the dog and
wrestles it.*

DANTE
Next time, I get the bed.

He releases the dog and sits up.

DANTE
(exhausted)
Shit.

Cut to:

INT: BATHROOM. MINUTES LATER

*A steaming shower fills the room. The dog licks water from the toilet. Cut
to:*

INT: KITCHEN. MINUTES LATER

A towel-dressed DANTE *opens the fridge and peers inside. He grabs a
half-empty gallon of milk and closes the door. Cut to:*

INT: KITCHEN. SECONDS LATER

*Chocolate milk mix is heaped into a tumbler. One scoop, two scoops, three
scoops, four scoops. Cut to:*

INT: BEDROOM. A MINUTE LATER

DANTE *gulps his breakfast while feeling inside the closet for some
clothes. Some chocolate milk spills on the floor.* THE DOG *laps at the
small puddle of chocolate milk. Cut to:*

INT: HALLWAY. MINUTES LATER

DANTE'S *feet are hastily covered. A hand grabs keys from atop a VCR. Cut to:*

EXT: DRIVEWAY. MINUTES LATER

A car backs out of the driveway and speeds down the street. Cut to:

EXT: CONVENIENCE STORE. MORNING

The car pulls up, with a screech. Feet descend to the ground from the open door. Keys jam into a lock and pop it open. Cut to:

DANTE *lifts the metal shutter revealing the door. He opens it and grabs two bundles of papers, throwing them inside the store. Cut to:*

INT: CONVENIENCE STORE. MORNING

A very dark room barely lit by the daylight. Suddenly, the lights flick on, revealing the glorious interior of the convenience store. THE CAT *looks at* DANTE *as he passes the camera quickly.* THE PAPER BUNDLE *is snapped open with a knife. Newspapers slam into the appropriate racks. One rack remains empty. A coffee filter is placed in a metal pot. Ground coffee follows, and the mix is shoved into place in the coffeemaker. The switch is flicked and the machine comes to life. The empty newspaper rack with the heading* ASBURY PARK PRESS *seems out of place among all the other stacks of papers.* DANTE *rubs his chin and stares, puzzled. He rolls his eyes as it occurs to him.*

                                    DANTE
          Shit.

The register pops open, and a hand extracts a quarter. Cut to:

EXT: CONVENIENCE STORE. MORNING

POV: NEWSPAPER MACHINE

Through murky glass and thin metal grating, we see DANTE *approach. He stops and drops a quarter in the slot. He pulls the door down, finally allowing us a clear view as he reaches toward the camera.*

DANTE *pulls a stack of newspapers from the* Asbury Park Press *vending machine. He struggles to hold them all in one hand as he lets the door slam shut. He turns to walk away, but the sound of the quarter dropping into the change slot stops him. He takes a step back to grab the coin. Cut to:*

INT: CONVENIENCE STORE. MORNING

The papers drop into the once-empty rack with a resounding flop. The quarter drops back into the register drawer. Cut to:

EXT: CONVENIENCE STORE. MORNING

DANTE *tries to jam the key into the window shutter lock. He looks down at it.*

> DANTE
> Shit!

The lock is gummed up with gum or something hard and obtrusive like gum, preventing the key from being inserted. DANTE *looks around and kicks the shutter angrily. The car trunk pops open and a hand reaches inside, pulling out a folded white sheet. Cut to:*

INT: CONVENIENCE STORE. MORNING

A can of shoe polish is grabbed from the shelf. DANTE *dips his fingers into the shoe polish and writes large letters on the unfurled sheet, leaning on the cooler. Cut to:*

EXT: CONVENIENCE STORE. MORNING

DANTE *stands on a garbage can and tucks a corner of the sheet under the awning. He jumps down. The banner reads* I ASSURE YOU, WE'RE OPEN. *The door sign shifts from* CLOSED *to* OPEN. *Cut to:*

INT: CONVENIENCE STORE. MORNING

The clock reads 6:20. DANTE *leans behind the counter, the morning routine completed. He stares ahead, catatonic, then drops his head in his hands. The day has begun. Cut to:*

EXT: CONVENIENCE STORE. DAY

The store, with its makeshift banner looming in the dim morning hour, just after dawn. A car drives by. Cut to:

INT: CONVENIENCE STORE. DAY

DANTE *waits on a customer* (ACTIVIST) *buying coffee.*

> DANTE
> Thanks. Have a good one.

> ACTIVIST
> Do you mind if I drink this here?

> DANTE
> Sure. Go ahead.

The ACTIVIST *leans on a briefcase and drinks his coffee. Another* CUSTOMER *leans in the door.*

> CUSTOMER
> Are you open?

> DANTE
> Yeah.

> CUSTOMER
> Pack of cigarettes.

> ACTIVIST
> Are you sure?

> CUSTOMER
> Am I sure?

> ACTIVIST
> Are you sure?

> CUSTOMER
> Am I sure about what?

> ACTIVIST
> Do you really want to buy those cigarettes?

CUSTOMER
Are you serious?

ACTIVIST
How long have you been smoking?

CUSTOMER
(to DANTE)
What is this, a poll?

DANTE
Beats me.

ACTIVIST
How long have you been a smoker?

CUSTOMER
Since I was thirteen.

The ACTIVIST *lifts his briefcase onto the counter. He opens it and extracts a sickly-looking lung model.*

ACTIVIST
I'd say you're about nineteen, twenty, am I right?

CUSTOMER

What in the hell is that?

ACTIVIST

That's your lung. By this time, your lung looks like this.

CUSTOMER

You're shittin' me.

ACTIVIST

You think I'm shitting you . . .

The ACTIVIST *hands him something from the briefcase.*

CUSTOMER

What's this?

ACTIVIST

It's a trach ring. It's what they install in your throat when throat cancer takes your voice box. This one came out of a sixty-year-old man.

CUSTOMER
(drops ring)

Unnhh!

ACTIVIST
(picks up the ring)

He smoked until the day he died. Used to put the cigarette in this thing and smoke it that way.

DANTE

Excuse me, but . . .

ACTIVIST

This is where you're heading. A cruddy lung, smoking through a hole in your throat. Do you really want that?

CUSTOMER

Well, if it's already too late . . .

ACTIVIST

It's never too late. Give those cigarettes back now, and buy some gum instead.
(grabs nearby pack, reads)
Here. Chewlies Gum. Try this.

CUSTOMER

It's not the same.

ACTIVIST

It's cheaper than cigarettes. And it certainly beats this.

Hands him a picture.

CUSTOMER

Jesus!

ACTIVIST

It's a picture of a cancer-ridden lung. Keep it.

CUSTOMER
(*to* DANTE)

I'll just take the gum.

DANTE

Fifty-five.

ACTIVIST

You've made a wise choice. Keep up the good work.

The CUSTOMER *exits.*

DANTE

Maybe you should take that coffee outside.

ACTIVIST

No, I think I'll drink it in here, thanks.

DANTE

If you're going to drink it in here, I'd appreciate it if you'd not bother the customers.

ACTIVIST

Okay. I'm sorry about that.

Another CUSTOMER *comes up to the counter.*

CUSTOMER

Pack of cigarettes.
                    (*looks at model*)
What's that?

ACTIVIST

This? How long have you been smoking?

Cut to:

EXT: CONVENIENCE STORE. DAY

A blank wall. JAY *steps into the frame, followed by* SILENT BOB. JAY
pulls off his coat and swings it into the arms of SILENT BOB. JAY *then
throws down with a makeshift slam dance, spinning his arm and fake-
hitting* SILENT BOB.

JAY

WE NEED SOME TITS AND ASS! YEAH!

SILENT BOB *lights a smoke.*

JAY

I feel good today, Silent Bob. We're gonna make some money!
And then you know what we're going to do? We're going to go
to that party and get some pussy! I'm gonna fuck this bitch, that
bitch . . .
                    (Blue Velvet *Hopper*)
I'LL FUCK ANYTHING THAT MOVES!

SILENT BOB *points to something off-screen.*

JAY
                    (*to OC*)
What you looking at?! I'll kick your fucking ass!
                    (*to* SILENT BOB)
Doesn't that motherfucker still owe me ten bucks?

SILENT BOB *nods.*

JAY

Tonight, you and me are going to rip off that fucker's head, and
take out his fucking soul! Remind me if he tries to buy something

from us, to cut it with leafs and twigs . . . or fucking shit in the motherfucker's bag!

Some girls walk past. JAY *smiles at them.*

JAY

Wa sup sluts?

(*to* SILENT BOB)

Damn Silent Bob! You one rude motherfucker! But you're cute as hell.

(*slowly drops to knees*)

I wanna go down on you, and suckle you.

(*makes blow job neck-jerks*)

And then, I wanna line up three more guys, and make like a circus seal . . .

JAY makes blow job faces down an imaginary line of guys, looking quite like a performing seal. He throws a little humming sound behind each nod. He then hops up quickly.

JAY

Ewwww! You fucking faggot! I fucking hate guys!

(*yelling*)

I LOVE WOMEN!

(*calmer*)

Neh.

A GUY comes up to them.

> GUY
>
> You selling?

> JAY
> *(all business)*
>
> I got hits, hash, weed, and later on I'll have 'shrooms. We take cash, or stolen MasterCard and Visa.

Cut to:

INT: CONVENIENCE STORE. DAY

A SMALL CROWD gathers around the ACTIVIST as he orates. It has become something of a rally.

> ACTIVIST
>
> You're spending what? Twenty, thirty dollars a week on cigarettes.

> LISTENER 1
>
> Forty.

> LISTENER 2
>
> Fifty-three.

ACTIVIST
Fifty-three dollars. Would you pay someone that much money
every week to kill you? Because that's what you're doing now,
by paying for the so-called privilege to smoke!

LISTENER 3
We all gotta go sometime . . .

ACTIVIST
It's that kind of mentality that allows this cancer-producing
industry to thrive. Of course we're all going to die someday, but
do we have to pay for it? Do we have to actually throw hard-
earned dollars on a counter and say, "Please, please, Mister
Merchant of Death, sir; please sell me something that will give
me bad breath, stink up my clothes, and fry my lungs."

LISTENER 1
It's not that easy to quit.

ACTIVIST
Of course it's not; not when you have people like this mindless
cretin so happy and willing to sell you nails for your coffin!

DANTE
Hey, now wait a sec . . .

ACTIVIST

Now he's going to launch into his rap about how he's just doing
his job; following orders. Friends, let me tell you about another
bunch of hate mongers that were just following orders: they were
called Nazis, and they practically wiped a nation of people from
the Earth . . . just like cigarettes are doing now! Cigarette smoking
is the new Holocaust, and those that partake in the practice of
smoking or sell the wares that promote it are the Nazis of the
nineties! He doesn't care how many people die from it! He smiles
as you pay for your cancer sticks and says, "Have a nice day."

DANTE

I think you'd better leave now.

ACTIVIST

You want me to leave? Why? Because somebody is telling it like
it is? Somebody's giving these fine people a wake-up call?!

DANTE

You're loitering in here, and causing a disturbance.

ACTIVIST

You're the disturbance, pal! And here . . . *(slaps a dollar on the
counter)* I'm buying some . . . what's this? . . . Chewlie's Gum.
There. I'm no longer loitering. I'm a customer, a customer
engaged in a discussion with other customers.

LISTENER 2
(to DANTE)

Yeah, now shut up so he can speak!

ACTIVIST

Oh, he's scared now! He sees the threat we present! He smells the
changes coming, and the loss of sales when the nonsmokers
finally demand satisfaction. We demand the right to breathe
cleaner air!

LISTENER 3

Yeah!

ACTIVIST

We'd rather chew our gum than embrace slow death! Let's
abolish this heinous practice of sucking poison, and if it means
ruffling the feathers of a convenience store idiot, then so be it!

                        DANTE
That's it, everybody out.

                        ACTIVIST
We're not moving! We have a right, a constitutional right, to
assemble and be heard!

                        DANTE
Yeah, but not in here.

                        ACTIVIST
What better place than this? To stamp it out, you gotta start at the
source!

                        DANTE
Like I'm responsible for all the smokers!

                        ACTIVIST
The ones in this town, yes! You encourage their growth, their
habit. You're the source in this area, and we're going to shut you
down for good! For good, cancer-merchant!

The small crowd begins to chant and jeer in DANTE's face.

                        CROWD
Cancer merchant! Cancer merchant! Cancer merchant!

*VERONICA enters and surveys the mess. The CROWD throws cigarettes
at DANTE, pelting him in the face. Suddenly, a loud blast is heard, and
white powder explodes over the throng. Everyone turns to face . . .*

*VERONICA as she stands on one of the freezer cases, holding a fire
extinguisher.*

                        VERONICA
Who's leading this mob?

The CROWD looks among themselves. Someone points to OC.

                        SOMEONE
    That guy.

The ACTIVIST carries his briefcase surreptitiously toward the door.

                              (OC) VERONICA
       Freeze.

VERONICA *jumps off the freezer case, training the nozzle of the*
extinguisher on the ACTIVIST.

                               VERONICA
       Let's see some credentials.

He reaches into his briefcase. She pokes the extinguisher nozzle at him,
warningly.

              Slowly . . .

He pulls out a business card and hands it to her. She reads it.

              You're a Chewlie's Gum representative?

He nods.

              And you're stirring up all this antismoking sentiment to . . . what?
              . . . sell more gum?

He nods again.

                          (through gritted teeth)

              Get out of here.

He quickly flees. She blasts him with more chemical as he exits.

                          (to the crowd)

              And you people: Don't you have jobs to go to?
              Get out of here and go commute.

The CROWD *sheepishly exits, one by one, offering apologetic glances.*
DANTE *tries to regain his composure.* VERONICA *watches the crowd*
disperse, disgusted.

              You oughta be ashamed of yourselves. Easily led automatons. Try
              thinking for yourselves before you pelt an innocent man with
              cigarettes.

The last of the crowd exits. VERONICA *sets the fire extinguisher down next to* DANTE. DANTE *is sitting on the floor, head in his folded arms.*

It looked like Tiananmen Square in here for a second.

DANTE *is silent.*

"Thank you, Veronica; you saved me from an extremely ugly mob scene."

DANTE *remains silent.*

(sits beside him)

Okay, champ. What's wrong?

DANTE *lifts his head and shoots her a disgusted look.*

All right, stupid question. But don't you think you're taking this a bit too hard?

DANTE
Too hard?! I don't have enough indignities in my life—people start throwing cigarettes at me!

VERONICA
At least they weren't lit.

DANTE
I hate this fucking place.

VERONICA
Then quit. You should be going to school anyway . . .

DANTE
Please, Veronica. Last thing I need is a lecture at this point.

VERONICA
All I'm saying is that if you're unhappy you should leave.

DANTE
I'm not even supposed to be here today!

VERONICA

I know. I stopped by your house and your mom said you left at like six or something.

DANTE

The guy got sick and couldn't come in.

VERONICA

Don't you have a hockey game at two?

DANTE

Yes! And I'm going to play like shit because I didn't get a good night's sleep!

VERONICA

Why did you agree to come in then?

DANTE

I'm only here until twelve, then I'm gone. The boss is coming in.

VERONICA

Why don't you open the shutters and get some sunlight in here?

DANTE

Somebody jammed the locks with gum.

VERONICA

You're kidding.

DANTE

Bunch of savages in this town.

VERONICA

You look bushed. What time did you get to bed?

DANTE

I don't know—like two-thirty, three.

VERONICA

What were you doing up so late?

DANTE
(skirting)

Hunhh? Nothing.

VERONICA
(persistent)
What were you doing?

DANTE
Nothing! Jesus! I gotta fight with you now?

VERONICA
Who's fighting? Why are you so defensive?

DANTE
Who's defensive? Just . . . Would you just hug me?! All right?
Your boyfriend was accosted by an angry mob, and he needs to
be hugged.

She stares at him.

DANTE
What? What is that?

VERONICA
She called you, didn't she?

DANTE
Oh, be real! Would you . . . Would you please hug me? I just went
through a very traumatic experience and I haven't been having
the best day so far. Now come on.

VERONICA *stares at him.*

DANTE
What? What's with that look?! I wasn't talking to anyone,
especially her! Look at you, being all sort of . . . I don't know . . .
stand-offish.

VERONICA *looks away.*

DANTE
Fine. You don't trust me, don't hug me. I see how it is. All right
Pissy-pants, you just go on being suspicious and quiet. I don't
even want to hug you at this point.

VERONICA *looks back at him.*

DANTE
(pleadingly)
Give you a dollar?

Cut to:

INT: CONVENIENCE STORE. DAY

A NOTE *on the counter next to a small pile of money reads:*

> PLEASE LEAVE MONEY ON THE COUNTER. TAKE CHANGE WHEN
> APPLICABLE. BE HONEST.

DANTE *and* VERONICA *are slumped on the floor, behind the counter.*
VERONICA *holds* DANTE *in her arms, his head on her chest. Change is
heard hitting the counter.*

DANTE
(to OC customer)
Thanks.

The door is heard opening and closing—a customer leaving.

VERONICA
How much money did you leave up there?

DANTE
Like three dollars in mixed change and a couple of singles. People
only get the paper or coffee this time of morning.

VERONICA
You're trusting.

DANTE
Why do you say that?

VERONICA
How do you know they're taking the right amount of change? Or
even paying for what they take?

DANTE
Theoretically, people see money on the counter and nobody
around, they think they're being watched.

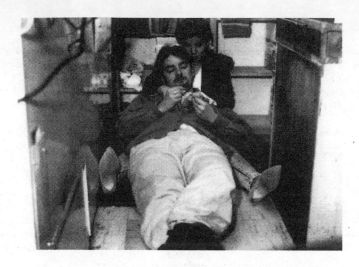

VERONICA

Honesty through paranoia. Why do you smell like shoe polish?

DANTE

I had to use shoe polish to make that sign. The smell won't come off.

VERONICA

Do you think anyone can see us down here?

DANTE

Why? You wanna have sex or something?

VERONICA
(sarcastic)

Ooh! Can we?!

DANTE

Really?

VERONICA

I was kidding.

DANTE

Yeah, right. You can't get enough of me.

VERONICA

Typically male point of view.

DANTE

How do you figure?

VERONICA

You show some bedroom proficiency, and you think you're gods.
What about what we do for you?

DANTE

Women? Women, as lovers, are all basically the same: they just
have to be there.

VERONICA

"Be there?"

DANTE

Making a male climax is not all that challenging: insert
somewhere close and preferably moist; thrust; repeat.

VERONICA

How flattering.

DANTE

Now, making a woman cum . . . therein lies a challenge.

VERONICA

Oh, you think so?

DANTE

A girl makes a guy cum, it's standard. A guy makes a girl cum,
it's talent.

VERONICA

And I actually date you?

DANTE

Something wrong?

VERONICA

I'm insulted. Believe me, Don Juan, it takes more than that to get
a guy off. Just "being there"—as you put it—is not enough.

DANTE

I touched a nerve.

VERONICA

I'm astonished to hear you trivialize my role in our sex life.

DANTE

It wasn't directed at you. I was making a broad generalization.

VERONICA

You were making a generalization about ''broads''!

DANTE

These are my opinions based on my experiences with the few
women who were good enough to sleep with me.

VERONICA

How many?

DANTE

How many what?

VERONICA

How many girls have you slept with?

DANTE

How many different girls? Didn't we already have this discussion
once?

VERONICA

We might have; I don't remember. How many?

DANTE

Including you?

VERONICA

It better be up to and including me.

DANTE
(pause to count)

Twelve.

VERONICA

You've slept with twelve different girls?

DANTE
Including you; yes.

Pause. She slaps him.

DANTE
What the hell was that for?

VERONICA
You're a pig.

DANTE
Why'd you hit me?

VERONICA
Do you know how many different men I've had sex with?

DANTE
Do I get to hit you after you tell me?

VERONICA
Three.

DANTE
Three?

VERONICA
Three including you.

DANTE
You've only had sex with three different people?

VERONICA
I'm not the pig you are.

DANTE
Who?

VERONICA
You!

DANTE
No; who were the three, besides me?

VERONICA
John Franson and Rob Stanslyk.

DANTE
(with true admiration)
Wow. That's great. That's something to be proud of.

VERONICA
I am. And that's why you should feel like a pig. You men make me sick. You'll sleep with anything that says yes.

DANTE
Animal, vegetable, or mineral.

VERONICA
Vegetable meaning paraplegic.

DANTE
They put up the least amount of struggle.

VERONICA
After dropping a bombshell like that, you owe me. Big.

DANTE
All right. Name it.

VERONICA
I want you to come with me on Monday.

DANTE
Where?

VERONICA
To school. There's a seminar about getting back into a scholastic program after a lapse in enrollment.

DANTE
Can't we ever have a discussion without that coming up?

VERONICA
It's important to me, Dante. You have so much potential that just goes to waste in this pit. I wish you'd go back to school.

DANTE

Jesus, would you stop? You make my head hurt when you talk about this.

VERONICA *stands, letting* DANTE'S *head hit the floor.*

DANTE

Shit! Why are we getting up?

VERONICA

Unlike you, I have a class in forty-five minutes.

A handsome young man (WILLAM) *is standing at the counter.* VERONICA *reacts to him.*

VERONICA
(surprised)

Willam!

WILLAM

Ronnie! How are you? You work here now?

VERONICA
(locks arms with DANTE*)*

No, I'm just visiting my man.
(to DANTE*)*
Dante, this is Willam Black.
(to WILLAM*)*
This is Dante Hicks, my boyfriend.

DANTE

How are you? Just the soda?

WILLAM

And a pack of cigarettes.
(to VERONICA; *paying)*
Are you still going to Seton Hall?

VERONICA

No, I transferred into Monmouth this year. I was tired of missing him.
(squeezes DANTE'S *arm)*

WILLAM

Do you still talk to Sylvan?

VERONICA

I just talked to her on Monday. We still hang out on weekends.

WILLAM
(leaving)
That's cool. Well—you two lovebirds take it easy, all right?

VERONICA

I will. Take it easy.

WILLAM

Bye.
(exits)

VERONICA

Bye.
(to Dante)
That was Snowball.

DANTE

Why do you call him that?

VERONICA

Sylvan made it up. It's a blow job thing.

DANTE

What do you mean?

VERONICA

After he gets a blow job, he likes to have the cum spit back into his mouth while kissing. It's called snowballing.

DANTE

He requested this?

VERONICA

He gets off on it.

DANTE

Sylvan can be talked into anything.

VERONICA
Why do you say that?

DANTE
Like you said—she snowballed him.

VERONICA
Sylvan? No; I snowballed him.

DANTE
Yeah, right.

VERONICA
I'm serious. . . .

A moment of silence as DANTE'S *chuckles fade to comprehension.*

DANTE
You sucked that guy's dick?

VERONICA
Yeah. How do you think I knew he liked . . .

DANTE
(panicky)
But . . . but you said you only had sex with three
guys! You never mentioned him!

VERONICA
That's because I never had sex with him!

DANTE
You sucked his dick!

VERONICA
We went out a few times. We didn't have sex, but we fooled
around.

DANTE
(massive panic attack)
Oh my God! Why did you tell me you only slept with three guys?

VERONICA

Because I did only sleep with three guys! That doesn't mean I didn't just go with people.

DANTE

Oh my God—I feel so nauseous . . .

VERONICA

I'm sorry, Dante. I thought you understood.

DANTE

I did understand! I understood that you slept with three different guys, and that's all you said.

VERONICA

Please calm down.

DANTE

How many?

VERONICA

Dante . . .

DANTE

How many dicks have you sucked?!

VERONICA

Let it go . . .

DANTE

HOW MANY?

VERONICA

All right! Shut up a second and I'll tell you! Jesus! I didn't freak like this when you told me how many girls you fucked.

DANTE

This is different. This is important. How many?!

She counts silently, using fingers as marks. DANTE *waits on a customer in the interim.* VERONICA *stops counting.*

DANTE

Well . . . ?

VERONICA
(half-mumbled)
Something like thirty-six.

DANTE
WHAT? SOMETHING LIKE THIRTY-SIX?

VERONICA
Lower your voice!

DANTE
What the hell is that anyway, "something like thirty-six"? Does that include me?

VERONICA
Um. Thirty-seven.

DANTE
I'M THIRTY-SEVEN?

VERONICA
(walking away)
I'm going to class.

DANTE
Thirty-seven?!
(to CUSTOMER)
My girlfriend sucked thirty-seven dicks!

CUSTOMER
In a row?

DANTE *chases* VERONICA *down and grabs her by the door.*

DANTE
Hey! Where are you going?!

VERONICA
Hey listen, jerk! Until today you never even knew how many guys I'd slept with, because you never even asked. And then you act all nonchalant about fucking twelve different girls. Well, I never had sex with twelve different guys!

DANTE

No, but you sucked enough dick!

VERONICA

Yeah, I went down on a few guys . . .

DANTE

A few?

VERONICA

. . . And one of those guys was you! The last one, I might add,
which—if you're too stupid to comprehend—means that I've
been faithful to you since we met! All the other guys I went with
before I met you, so, if you want to have a complex about it, go
ahead! But don't look at me like I'm the town whore, because
you were plenty busy yourself, before you met me!

DANTE
(a bit more rational)

Well . . . why did you have to suck their dicks? Why didn't you
just sleep with them, like any decent person?!

VERONICA

Because going down isn't a big deal! I used to like a guy, we'd
make out, and sooner or later I'd go down on him. But I only had
sex with the guys I loved.

DANTE

I feel sick.

VERONICA
(holds him)

I love you. Don't feel sick.

DANTE

Every time I kiss you now I'm going to taste thirty-six other guys.

VERONICA *violently lets go of him.*

VERONICA

I'm going to school. Maybe later you'll be a bit more rational.

                    DANTE
                   (pause)
Thirty-seven. I just can't . . .

                    VERONICA
Goodbye, Dante.

She exits in a huff. DANTE stands there in silence for a moment. Then he swings the door open and yells out.

                    DANTE
Try not to suck any more dicks on your way through the parking lot!

Two men who were walking in the opposite direction outside double back and head in the direction VERONICA went.

                    DANTE
HEY! HEY, YOU! GET BACK HERE!

Cut to:

INT: CONVENIENCE STORE. DAY

A videocassette encased in the customary black box flips repeatedly, held by an impatient grasp. The IMPATIENT CUSTOMER glares at DANTE. Dante studies a copy of Paradise Lost, *making a strong attempt at not noticing the glare.*

                    IMPATIENT CUSTOMER
                   (pissed off)
I thought that place was supposed to be opened at eleven o'clock? It's twenty after!

                    DANTE
I called his house twice already. He should be here soon.

                    IMPATIENT CUSTOMER
It's not like it's a demanding job. I'd like to get paid to sit on my ass and watch TV. The other day I walked in there and that sonofabitch was sleeping.

                    DANTE
I'm sure he wasn't sleeping.

IMPATIENT CUSTOMER
You calling me a liar?

DANTE
No; he was probably just resting his eyes.

IMPATIENT CUSTOMER
What the hell is that? Resting his eyes! It's not like he's some goddamned air traffic controller!

DANTE
Actually, that's his night job.

IMPATIENT CUSTOMER
Such a wiseass. But go ahead. Crack wise. That's why you're jockeying a register in some fucking local convenience store instead of doing an honest day's work.
(tosses tape on counter)
I got no more time to bullshit around waiting for that sonofabitch. You make sure this gets back. The number's eight-twelve—Wynarski. And I wanted to get a damn movie, too.

DANTE
If you'll just tell me the title of your rental choice, I'll have him hold it for you.

IMPATIENT CUSTOMER
(storming out)
Don't hurt yourself. I'm going to Big Choice Video instead.

He storms out. Dante lifts a ring of keys from the counter.

DANTE
(in a whisper)
You forgot your keys.

The half-filled trash can swallows the ring of keys. Cut to:

EXT: CONVENIENCE STORE. DAY

Another VIDEO-ANXIOUS CUSTOMER *leans against the video store door. A hapless* RANDAL *drifts by and stops. He glances at the door, peers inside, and gives the door a tug.*

                    V.A. CUSTOMER
The guy ain't here yet.

                    RANDAL
You're kidding. It's almost eleven-thirty!

                    V.A. CUSTOMER
I know. I've been here since eleven.

                    RANDAL
                    (kicks the door)
Man! I hate it when I can't rent videos!

                    V.A. CUSTOMER
I would've went to Big Choice, but the tape I want is right there
on the wall.

                    RANDAL
Which one?

                    V.A. CUSTOMER
Dental School.

                    RANDAL
You came for that too? That's the movie I came for.

                    V.A. CUSTOMER
I have first dibs.

                    RANDAL
Says who?

                    V.A. CUSTOMER
                    (suddenly snotty)
Says me. I've been here for half an hour. I'd call that first dibs.

                    RANDAL
Ain't gonna happen, my friend. I'm getting that tape.

                    V.A. CUSTOMER
Like hell you are!

                    RANDAL
I'll bet you twenty bucks you don't get to rent that tape.

V.A. CUSTOMER
Twenty bucks?

RANDAL
Twenty bucks.

V.A. CUSTOMER
All right, asshole, you're on.

RANDAL *walks away. The* VERY ANXIOUS CUSTOMER *stands like a sentry at post. The* IMPATIENT CUSTOMER *storms up.*

IMPATIENT CUSTOMER
You see a pair of keys lying around here somewhere?

Cut to:

INT: CONVENIENCE STORE. DAY

RANDAL *dances in, attempting a soft-shoe routine. He sees* DANTE *and stops dead, midshuffle.*

DANTE
You're late.

RANDAL
What the hell are you doing here? I thought you were playing hockey at one.

DANTE
The boss called. Arthur fell ill.

RANDAL
Why are the shutters closed?

DANTE
Someone jammed gum in the locks.

RANDAL
Bunch of savages in this town.

DANTE
That's what I said.

RANDAL

Shit, if I'd known you were working, I would've come even later.

A pile of videocassettes is plopped onto the counter, with a single key on top. RANDAL balances the pile of tapes on his head.

RANDAL

What time do you have to stay till?

DANTE

He assured me that he'd be here by twelve.

RANDAL

What smells like shoe polish?

DANTE

Go open the store.

Cut to:

EXT: CONVENIENCE STORE. DAY

The IMPATIENT CUSTOMER stops RANDAL.

IMPATIENT CUSTOMER

Hey—did you see a set of keys lying around here?

RANDAL
(as Short-round)

No time for love, Doctor Jones!

RANDAL marches off. The IMPATIENT CUSTOMER stares after him.

IMPATIENT CUSTOMER

Fucking kids.

The VERY ANXIOUS CUSTOMER now sits on the ground, next to the video store door. RANDAL balances his burden and shoves the key into the lock. The VERY ANXIOUS CUSTOMER stares as RANDAL enters the store. The door closes behind him, only to be held ajar in a gentlemanly fashion a few moments later. RANDAL smiles. Cut to:

INT: CONVENIENCE STORE. DAY

A coffee filter is shoved into the metal pan and someone heaps ground coffee on it. We've seen this same routine before. DANTE crosses back to his post, as RANDAL enters, tossing the key into the air happily and catching it. He picks the cat up.

> RANDAL
> Some guy just came in refusing to pay late fees. He said the store was closed for two hours yesterday. I tore up his membership.

> DANTE
> Shocking abuse of authority.

> RANDAL
> I'm a firm believer in the philosophy of a ruling class, especially since I rule.
> *(furtively)*
> Is the Pelican flying?

> DANTE
> Don't screw with it. It makes us look suspicious.

> RANDAL
> I can't stand a voyeur. I'll be back.

RANDAL heads toward the walk-in door. Cut to:

INT: BACK ROOM. DAY

POV: VCR

A far-away wall is the only thing we see, but mild gruntings give away an ascension of sorts. RANDAL'S head rises into view, as if he's climbing a ladder. He stops and looks into the lens.

POV: RANDAL
The PELICAN is a VCR that's hooked up to a surveillance camera. It records quickly. A hand reaches into the frame and shuts it off. Cut to:

INT: CONVENIENCE STORE. DAY

RANDAL pulls a soda from the cooler.

                              RANDAL
Want something to drink? I'm buying.

                            (OC) DANTE
No, thanks.

                              RANDAL
Who was on your phone this morning at about two-thirty? I was
trying to call for a half an hour.

                            (OC) DANTE
Why?

                              RANDAL
I wanted to use your car.

He walks by a row of snacks and grabs one without looking at it.

                              RANDAL
Snack cake?

DANTE *sits in his seat behind the register.* RANDAL *grabs a paper and
joins him behind the counter.*

                              DANTE
You don't want to know.

                              RANDAL
You called Caitlin again?!

                              DANTE
She called me.

                              RANDAL
Did you tell Veronica?

                              DANTE
One fight a day with Veronica is about all I can stomach, thanks.

                              RANDAL
What do you two fight about?

DANTE

I guess it's not really fighting. She just wants me to leave here, go back to school, get some direction.

RANDAL
(opening paper)

I'll bet the most frequent topic of arguments is Caitlin Bree.

DANTE

You win.

RANDAL

I'm going to offer you some advice, my friend: let the past be the past. Forget Caitlin Bree. You've been with Veronica for how long now?

DANTE

Seven months.

RANDAL

Chick's nuts about you. How long did you date Caitlin?

DANTE

Five years.

RANDAL

Chick only made you nuts. She cheated on you how many times?

DANTE

Eight and a half.

RANDAL
(looks up from paper)

Eight and a half?

DANTE

Party at John K's—senior year. I get blitzed and pass out in his bedroom. Caitlin comes in and dives all over me.

RANDAL

That's cheating?

DANTE

In the middle of it, she calls me Brad.

RANDAL

She called you Brad?

DANTE

She called me Brad.

RANDAL

That's not cheating. People say crazy shit during sex. One time, I
called this girl "Mom."

DANTE

I hit the lights and she freaks. Turns out she thought I was Brad
Michaelson.

RANDAL

What do you mean?

DANTE

She was supposed to meet Brad Michaelson in a bedroom. She
picked the wrong one. She had no idea I was even at the party.

RANDAL

Oh, my God.

DANTE

Great story, isn't it?

RANDAL

That girl was vile to you.

DANTE

Interesting postscript to that story: Do you know who wound up
going with Brad Michaelson in the other dark bedroom?

RANDAL

Your mother.

DANTE

Allan Harris.

RANDAL

Chess team Allan Harris?!

DANTE

The two moved to Idaho together after graduation. They raise
sheep.

RANDAL

That's frightening.

DANTE

It takes different strokes to move the world.

RANDAL

In light of this lurid tale, I don't see how you could even
romanticize your relationship with Caitlin—she broke your heart
and inadvertently drove men to deviant lifestyles.

DANTE

Because there was a lot of good in our relationship.

RANDAL

Oh yeah.

DANTE

I'm serious. Aside from the cheating, we were a great couple.
That's what high school's all about—algebra, bad lunch, and
infidelity.

RANDAL

You think things would be any different now?

DANTE

They are. When she calls me now, she's a different person—she's
frightened and vulnerable. She's about to finish college and enter
the real world. That's got to be scary for anyone.

RANDAL
(suddenly recalling)
Oh shit, I've got to place an order.

DANTE

I'm talking to myself here.

RANDAL

No, no, I'm listening. She's leaving college, and . . . ?

DANTE

... and she's looking to me for support. And I think that this is leading our relationship to a new level.

RANDAL

What about Veronica?

DANTE

I think the arguments Veronica and I are having are some kind of manifestation of a subconscious desire to break away from her so that I can pursue the possibility of a more meaningful relationship with Caitlin.

RANDAL

Caitlin's on the same wave-length?

DANTE

I think it's safe to say yes.

RANDAL

Then I think all four of you had better sit down and talk it over.

DANTE

All four?

RANDAL

You, Veronica, Caitlin . . .
(lays paper flat)
. . . and Caitlin's fiancé.

THE HEADLINE of the engagement announcement reads, BREE TO WED ASIAN DESIGN MAJOR.

Cut to:

INT: VIDEO STORE. DAY

RANDAL dials the phone. He holds a list in his hand.

RANDAL

Yes, I'd like to place an order, please . . . Thank you.

A MOTHER *and her* SMALL CHILD *approach the counter.*

MOTHER

Excuse me, but do you sell videotapes?

RANDAL

What were you looking for?

MOTHER
(smiling)

It's called *Happy Scrappy—The Hero Pup.*

SMALL CHILD

Happy Scrappy!

RANDAL

I'm on the phone with the distribution house now. Let me make sure they have it. What's it called again?

MOTHER

Happy Scrappy—The Hero Pup.

SMALL CHILD

Happy Scrappy!

MOTHER
(more smiling)

She loves the tape.

RANDAL

Obviously.
(to phone)
Yes, hello; this is R.S.T. Video calling. Customer number four-three-five-zero-two-nine. I'd like to place an order . . . Okay . . .
(reading from list)
I need one each of the following tapes: *Whisper in the Wind, To Each His Own, Put it Where It Doesn't Belong, My Pipes Need Cleaning, All Tit-Fucking, Volume Eight, I Need Your Cock, Ass-Worshipping Rim-Jobbers, My Cunt and Eight Shafts, Cum Clean, Cum-Gargling Naked Sluts, Cum Buns Three, Cumming in a Sock, Cum on Eileen, Huge Black Cocks with Pearly White Cum, Slam It Up My Too-Loose Ass, Ass Blasters in Outer Space, Blowjobs by Betsy, Sucking Cock and Cunt, Finger My Ass, Play with my Puss, Three on a Dildo, Girls Who Crave Cock, Girls*

Who Crave Cunt, Men Alone Two—The K.Y. Connection, Pink
Pussy Lips, and All Holes Filled with Hard Cock. Oh, and . . .
                    (to MOTHER)
What was the name of that movie?

                    MOTHER
                  (nearly dazed)
Happy Scrappy—The Hero Pup.

                    RANDAL
                  (to phone)
And a copy of *Happy Scrappy—The Hero Pup* . . . Okay, thanks.
          (hangs up; to MOTHER)
Sixteen forty-nine. It'll be here Monday.

Silence. Then . . .

                    SMALL CHILD
Cunt!

Cut to:

INT: CONVENIENCE STORE. DAY

DANTE *carries a litter box to be dumped. He pauses midstride and lays
it on the ice cream chest.* DANTE *picks up the phone and looks at the
paper. He dials and waits.*

                    DANTE
Yes, I'd like to check on a misprint in today's edition . . . Today's
edition . . . It says "Bree to Wed Asian Design Major . . . No, no;
everything's spelled fine. I just wanted to know if the piece was a
misprint . . . I don't know, like a typographical error or
something . . .

A CUSTOMER *comes to the counter and waits. He looks at the litter box.
A black cat suddenly jumps into it and starts pawing around.*

                    (OC) DANTE
Maybe it's supposed to be Caitlin Bray, or Caitlin Bre, with one
e . . . I'm a curious party . . . A curious party . . .

DANTE *on the phone:*

DANTE

. . . I'm an ex-boyfriend . . . Well, it's just that we talk all the time, and she never mentioned this engagement, which is why I'm thinking maybe it's a misprint . . .

The CUSTOMER *watches as the cat takes a huge dump, leaning high on its haunches to accommodate the stinky load.*

(OC) DANTE

. . . Are you sure? . . . Maybe there's like a vindictive printer working for you . . .

DANTE *on the phone*:

DANTE

Meaning like someone who maybe—I don't know—asked her out once and got shot down, and his revenge is throwing this bogus article in when the paper went to press . . . Hello? . . . Hello?

DANTE *hangs up. He looks at the paper ruefully, shaking his head. He then sniffs the air. Cut to:*

EXT: CONVENIENCE STORE. DAY

JAY, SILENT BOB *and* OLAF *lean against wall*

JAY

"Not in me." That's what she says. I gotta pull out and spank it to get it on. So I blow a nut on her belly, and I get out of there, just as my uncle walks in. It was such a close call. I tell you what, though, I don't care if she is my cousin, I'm gonna knock those boots again tonight.

TWO GIRLS *join them.*

JAY

Oh shit, look who it is. The human vacuum.

GIRL 1

Scumbag. What are you doing?

JAY

Nothing. Just hanging out, talking with Silent Bob and his cousin.

GIRL 1
(to SILENT BOB*)*

He's your cousin?

JAY

Check this out, he's from Russia.

GIRL 1

No way.

JAY

I swear to God. Silent Bob, am I lying?

SILENT BOB *shakes his head:*

JAY

See? And Silent Bob never told a lie in his life.

GIRL 2

What part of Russia?

JAY

I don't fucking know. What am I, his biographer?
(to OLAF*)*
Olaf, what part of Russia are you from?

OLAF *looks quizzically at* SILENT BOB.

SILENT BOB
(in Russian)

Home.

OLAF
(comprehending)

Moscow.

GIRL 1

He only speaks Russian?

JAY

He knows some English, but he can't not speak it good like we do.

GIRL 2

Is he staying here?

                    JAY

He's moving to the big city next week. He wants to be a metal
singer.

                   GIRL 1

No way!

                    JAY

Swear.
                  (to OLAF)
Olaf, metal!

OLAF *makes a metal face.*

                    JAY

That's his fucking metal face.
                  (to OLAF)
Olaf, girls nice?

OLAF *looks the girls up and down.*

                   OLAF

Skrelnick.

                    JAY
                  (laughs)
That's fucked up.

                   GIRL 1

What did he say?

                    JAY

I don't know, man. He's a fucking character.

                   GIRL 2

He really wants to play metal?

                    JAY

He's got his own band in Moscow. It's called "Fuck Your Yankee
Blue Jeans" or something like that.

                   GIRL 1

That doesn't sound metal.

                          JAY
        You gotta hear him sing.
                          (to OLAF)
        Olaf, ''Berserker''!

OLAF *laughs and shakes his head.*

                          JAY
        Come on, man, ''Berserker''!

                          GIRL 2
        Does he sing in English or Russian?

                          JAY
        English.
                          (to OLAF)
        Come on, ''Berserker''! Girls think sexy.

                          OLAF
                        (relents)
        Da. Da.

                          JAY
        He's gonna sing it. This is too funny.

                          OLAF
                      (in broken English)
        MY LOVE FOR YOU IS LIKE A TRUCK BERSERKER!
        WOULD YOU LIKE SOME MAKING FUCK?
        BERSERKER!

                          JAY
                       (laughing)
        That's fucking funny, man!

                          GIRL 1
        Did he say ''making fuck''?

                          JAY
        Wait, there's more.
                          (to OLAF)
        Olaf: sing . . .
                      (makes pot-smoking face)

OLAF
            (nods in understanding)
    MY LOVE FOR YOU IS LIKE A ROCK
    BERSERKER!
    WOULD YOU LIKE TO SMOKE SOME POT?
    BERSERKER!

OLAF *busts a crimson metal sneer and cackles deeply. Cut to:*

INT: VIDEO STORE. DAY

RANDAL *leans back in his chair, staring up at the TV. The theme to* Star
Wars *plays. He stands, points the remote, clicks the TV off, and ponders.
Cut to:*

EXT: VIDEO STORE. DAY

RANDAL *locks the door and walks away, while* OLAF *sings for the small
crowd.*

                    OLAF
    MY LOVE FOR YOU IS TICKING CLOCK
    BERSERKER!
    WOULD YOU LIKE TO SUCK MY COCK?
    BERSERKER!

Cut to:

INT: CONVENIENCE STORE. DAY

DANTE *is tugging at a can of Pringles potato chips. The can is stuck on a* MAN'S *hand.*

> DANTE
>
> You hold the counter and I'll pull.

> MAN
>
> Usually I just turn the can upside down.

> DANTE
> *(pulling)*
>
> Maybe we should soap up your hand or something.

> MAN
> *(straining)*
>
> They oughta put some kind of warning on these cans, like they do with cigarettes.

> DANTE
>
> I think it's coming now . . .

The can pops off and DANTE *staggers back a few steps. The man rubs his hand.*

> MAN
>
> Thanks. I thought I was gonna have to go to the hospital.

> DANTE
>
> I'll throw this out. Precautionary measure.

> MAN
>
> It stings a little.

> DANTE
>
> A word of advice: Sometimes it's best to let those hard to reach chips go.

DANTE *steps behind the counter.*

MAN

Thanks.

The MAN *exits as* RANDAL *enters.* DANTE *throws the canister away.*

DANTE

Do you know that article is accurate? Caitlin's really getting
married!

RANDAL

You know what I just watched?

DANTE

Me pulling a can off some moron's fist.

RANDAL

Return of the Jedi.

DANTE

Didn't you hear me? Caitlin really is getting married.

RANDAL

Which did you like better: *Jedi* or *The Empire Strikes Back*?

DANTE
(exasperated)

Empire.

RANDAL

Blasphemy.

DANTE

Empire had the better ending: Luke gets his hand cut off, and
finds out Vader's his father; Han gets frozen and taken away by
Boba Fett. It ends on such a down note. And that's life—a series
of down endings. All *Jedi* had was a bunch of Muppets.

RANDAL

There was something else going on in *Jedi.* I never noticed it until
today.

RANDAL *follows* DANTE *as he cleans up around the store.*

DANTE

What's that?

RANDAL

All right, Vader's boss . . .

DANTE

The Emperor.

RANDAL

Right, the Emperor. Now the Emperor is kind of a spiritual figure,
yes?

DANTE

How do you mean?

RANDAL

Well, he's like the pope for the dark side of the Force. He's a holy
man; a shaman, kind of, albeit an evil one.

DANTE

I guess.

RANDAL

Now, he's in charge of the Empire. The Imperial government is
under his control. And the entire galaxy is under Imperial rule.

DANTE

Yeah.

RANDAL

Then wouldn't that logically mean that it's a theocracy?
If the head of the Empire is a priest of some sort, then it stands to
reason that the government is therefore one based on religion.

DANTE

It would stand to reason, yes.

RANDAL

Hence, the Empire was a fascist theocracy, and the rebel forces
were therefore battling religious persecution.

DANTE

More or less.

RANDAL

The only problem is that at no point in the series did I ever hear
Leia or any of the rebels declare a particular religious belief.

DANTE

I think they were Catholics.

A BLUE-COLLAR MAN *half enters the door.*

BLUE-COLLAR MAN

Are you open?

DANTE

Yeah. Come in.

He goes to the coffee machine and makes a cup of joe.

RANDAL

You know what else I noticed in *Jedi*?

DANTE

There's more?

RANDAL

So they build another Death Star, right?

DANTE

Yeah.

RANDAL

Now the first one they built was completed and fully operational
before the Rebels destroyed it.

DANTE

Luke blew it up. Give credit where it's due.

RANDAL

And the second one was still being built when they blew it up.

DANTE

Compliments of Lando Calrissian.

RANDAL
Something just never sat right with me the second time they destroyed it. I could never put my finger on it—something just wasn't right.

DANTE
And you figured it out?

RANDAL
Well, the thing is, the first Death Star was manned by the Imperial army—storm troopers, dignitaries—the only people onboard were Imperials.

DANTE
Basically.

RANDAL
So when they blew it up, no prob. Evil is punished.

DANTE
And the second time around . . . ?

RANDAL
The second time around, it wasn't even finished yet. They were still under construction.

DANTE
So?

RANDAL
A construction job of that magnitude would require a helluva lot more manpower than the Imperial army had to offer. I'll bet there were independent contractors working on that thing: plumbers, aluminum siders, roofers.

DANTE
Not just Imperials, is what you're getting at.

RANDAL
Exactly. In order to get it built quickly and quietly they'd hire anybody who could do the job. Do you think the average storm trooper knows how to install a toilet main? All they know is killing and white uniforms.

DANTE

All right, so even if independent contractors are working on the Death Star, why are you uneasy with its destruction?

RANDAL

All those innocent contractors hired to do a job were killed—casualties of a war they had nothing to do with.
(notices Dante's *confusion)*
All right, look—you're a roofer, and some juicy government contract comes your way; you got the wife and kids and the two-story in suburbia—this is a government contract, which means all sorts of benefits. All of a sudden these left-wing militants blast you with lasers and wipe out everyone within a three-mile radius. You didn't ask for that. You have no personal politics. You're just trying to scrape out a living.

The BLUE-COLLAR MAN *joins them.*

BLUE-COLLAR MAN

Excuse me. I don't mean to interrupt, but what were you talking about?

RANDAL

The ending of *Return of the Jedi.*

DANTE

My friend is trying to convince me that any contractors working on the uncompleted Death Star were innocent victims when the space station was destroyed by the rebels.

BLUE-COLLAR MAN

Well, I'm a contractor myself. I'm a roofer . . .
(digs into pocket and produces business card)
Dunn and Reddy Home Improvements. And speaking as a roofer, I can say that a roofer's personal politics come heavily into play when choosing jobs.

RANDAL

Like when?

BLUE-COLLAR MAN

Three months ago I was offered a job up in the hills. A beautiful house with tons of property. It was a simple reshingling job, but

I was told that if it was finished within a day, my price would be doubled. Then I realized whose house it was.

                            DANTE
Whose house was it?

                    BLUE-COLLAR MAN
Dominick Bambino's.

                            RANDAL
"Babyface" Bambino? The gangster?

                    BLUE-COLLAR MAN
The same. The money was right, but the risk was too big. I knew who he was, and based on that, I passed the job on to a friend of mine.

                            DANTE
Based on personal politics.

                    BLUE-COLLAR MAN
Right. And that week, the Foresci family put a hit on Babyface's house. My friend was shot and killed. He wasn't even finished shingling.

                            RANDAL
No way!

                    BLUE-COLLAR MAN
                    (paying for coffee)
I'm alive because I knew there were risks involved taking on that particular client. My friend wasn't so lucky.
                    (pauses to reflect)
You know, any contracter willing to work on that Death Star knew the risks. If they were killed, it was their own fault. A roofer listens to this . . .
                    (taps his heart)
not his wallet.

The BLUE-COLLAR MAN *exits.* DANTE *and* RANDAL *remain respectfully quiet for a moment. An angry* WOMAN *opens the door and pokes her head in.*

Is that video store open or not?

Cut to:

INT: VIDEO STORE. DAY

RANDAL *reads a newspaper. An* INDECISIVE CUSTOMER *studies the two rental choices she holds. She looks from one movie to the other, repeatedly.*

> INDECISIVE CUSTOMER
> *(attempting to solicit help)*
> They say so much, but they never tell you if it's any good.

RANDAL *hardly stirs and continues to read his paper. The* INDECISIVE CUSTOMER *half turns to see if her comment was even heard. She tries again, but this time with a different approach.*

> INDECISIVE CUSTOMER
> Are either of these any good?

RANDAL *continues to read. The* INDECISIVE CUSTOMER *tries harder, then louder and more direct:*

Sir!

RANDAL *continues to read.*

> RANDAL
> *(flatly)*

What.

The INDECISIVE CUSTOMER *holds up her rental choices.*

> INDECISIVE CUSTOMER
> *(politely)*
> Are either of these any good?

RANDAL, *as always, reads on.*

RANDAL
(again, flatly)

I don't watch movies.

The INDECISIVE CUSTOMER *is a tad flabbergasted, but not put off.*

INDECISIVE CUSTOMER
Well, have you heard anything about either of them?

RANDAL *does his level best to not get involved.*

RANDAL
(reading)

No.

The INDECISIVE CUSTOMER *challenges him.*

INDECISIVE CUSTOMER
(in disbelief)
You've never heard anybody say anything about either movie?

(OC) RANDAL
I find it's best to stay out of other people's affairs.

INDECISIVE CUSTOMER
(with a new determination)
Well, how about these two movies?
(holds up the same two)

RANDAL *continues to read his paper, not looking up.*

RANDAL
They suck.

The INDECISIVE CUSTOMER *smirks smugly at* RANDAL *and his paper. She has caught him.*

INDECISIVE CUSTOMER
I just held up the same two movies. You're not even paying attention.

RANDAL
No, I wasn't.

INDECISIVE CUSTOMER
I don't think your manager would appreciate . . .

RANDAL
(turning the page)
I don't appreciate your ruse, ma'am.

INDECISIVE CUSTOMER
I beg your pardon!

RANDAL
(reading on)
Your ruse. Your cunning attempt to trick me.

INDECISIVE CUSTOMER
(defending herself)
I only pointed out that you weren't paying any attention to what I was saying.

RANDAL
(turning page and reading)
I hope it feels good.

INDECISIVE CUSTOMER
You hope what feels good?

RANDAL
I hope it feels so good to be right. There is nothing more exhilarating than pointing out the shortcomings of others, is there?

The INDECISIVE CUSTOMER *wears a face that belies utter disbelief in the audacity of this most lackadaisical video clerk. The unmoving newspaper illustrates the total disinterest of the news-hungry RANDAL. The* INDECISIVE CUSTOMER *shakes her head in digust and throws the movies back onto the wall.*

INDECISIVE CUSTOMER
(in a huff)
Well this is the last time I ever rent here . . .

RANDAL
You'll be missed.

INDECISIVE CUSTOMER
(losing it altogether)

Screw you!

She storms out. RANDAL is offended. He hops over the counter and whips the door open.

RANDAL
(calling after her)

You're not allowed to rent here anymore!

RANDAL closes the door and stands there, momentarily, totally appalled by her exiting remark, then shakes his head.

Screw me!

He reaches behind the counter and grabs a ring of keys. Exiting, he locks the door behind him from outside, gives it a tug to ensure its security, and storms off in the opposite direction from the woman. Cut to:

INT: CONVENIENCE STORE. DAY

DANTE is staring, open-mouthed, at something OC. RANDAL hurls the door open and immediately launches into his tirade.

RANDAL

You'll never believe what this unruly customer just said . . .

DANTE
(a hand up to urge him to hush)

Wait.

RANDAL
(looking around)

She's in here?

DANTE

This guy is going through all of the eggs. Look.

An ODD MAN sits on the floor, surrounded by cartons of eggs, all opened. He grabs a carton from the cooler case, pops it open, and examines each egg carefully.

(OC) DANTE
This has been going on for twenty minutes.

RANDAL *and* DANTE *study the OC oddity.*

RANDAL
What's he looking for?

DANTE
He said he has to find a perfect dozen.

RANDAL
Perfect dozen.

DANTE
Each egg has to be perfect.

RANDAL
The quest isn't going well?

DANTE
Obviously not. Look at all the cartons that didn't make the grade.

The ODD MAN *holds an egg up to the light and studies it from several different angles.*

(OC) RANDAL
Why doesn't he just mix and match?

(OC) DANTE
I told him that and he yelled at me.

RANDAL *snickers at his friend.*

RANDAL
What did he say?

DANTE
He said it was important to have standards. He said nobody has pride anymore.

RANDAL
It's not like you laid the eggs yourself.

DANTE

I'll give him five more minutes and then I'm calling the cops. I
don't need this, man. I'm not even supposed to be here today.

A SMOKER steps in.

SMOKER

Two packs of cigarettes.

*Dante manages to break his study of the OC oddity and searches for the
smokes. The smoker glances at RANDAL and then at the OC oddity.*

*The ODD MAN is spinning an egg on the floor. The SMOKER looks at
RANDAL.*

RANDAL
(still staring at the ODD MAN)
I'm as puzzled as you.

SMOKER
(paying DANTE)
I've actually seen it before.

DANTE

You know him?

SMOKER

No, I've seen that behavior before. Looking for the perfect carton
of eggs, right?

RANDAL
(a bit astonished)
Yeah. How'd you know?

SMOKER

I'll bet you a million bucks that the guy's a guidance counselor.

DANTE

Why do you say that?

SMOKER

I was in Food City last year when the same thing happened,
different guy though. Stock boy told me that the guy had been

looking through the eggs for like half an hour, doing all sorts of endurance tests and shit. I ask the kid how come nobody called the manager, and he says it happens twice a week, sometimes more.

> RANDAL

Get out of here.

> SMOKER

I kid you not. They call it Shell Shock. Only happens with guidance counselors for some reason. The kid said they used to make a big deal about it, but there's no point.

The ODD MAN places a handkerchief over an egg on the floor. He quickly whisks the handkerchief away to reveal the egg still sitting on the floor.

> (OC) SMOKER

He said they always pay for whatever they break and they never bother anybody.

DANTE, RANDAL *and the* SMOKER *stare at the OC man.*

> DANTE

Why guidance counselors?

> SMOKER

If your job served as little purpose as theirs, wouldn't you lose it, too?

> RANDAL

Come to think of it, my guidance counselor was kind of worthless.

> SMOKER
> *(grabbing matches)*

See? It's important to have a job that makes a difference, boys. That's why I kill Chinamen for the railroad.

Cut to:

INT: CONVENIENCE STORE. DAY

POV RANDAL: THE EMPTY COUNTER

And then a LITTLE GIRL *comes into view, smiling and holding money. She can't be any more than five.*

(innocently)
Can I have a pack of cigarettes?

RANDAL, *without looking up from his magazine, completes the transaction.* THE LITTLE GIRL *puts a cigarette in her mouth.* RANDAL *hands her matches.* DANTE *returns to the counter as the girl skips away. Dante holds a price gun.*

DANTE
Did you ever notice all the prices end in nine? Damn, that's eerie.

RANDAL
You know how much money the average jizz-mopper makes per hour?

DANTE
What's a jizz-mopper?

RANDAL
He's the guy in those nudie-booth joints who cleans up after each guy that jerks off.

DANTE
Nudie booth?

RANDAL
Nudie booth. You've never been in a nudie booth?

DANTE
I guess not.

A female CUSTOMER *pops items onto the counter.* DANTE *rings her up.*

RANDAL
Oh, it's great. You step into this little booth and there's this window between you and this naked woman, and she puts on this little show for like ten bucks.

DANTE
What kind of show?

RANDAL

Think of the weirdest, craziest shit you'd like to see chicks do.
These chicks do it all. They insert things into any opening in their
body . . . *any* opening.
(*to customer*)
He's led a very sheltered life.

DANTE
(*indicating* CUSTOMER)
Can we talk about this later?

RANDAL

The jizz-mopper's job is to clean up the booths afterward, because
practically everybody shoots a load against the window, and I
don't know if you know this or not, but cum leaves streaks if you
don't clean it right away.

CUSTOMER
(*grabbing her bag, disgusted*)
This is the last time I come to this place.

DANTE

Excuse me?

CUSTOMER

Using filthy language in front of the customers . . . you should
both get fired.

DANTE

We're sorry, ma'am. We got a little carried away.

CUSTOMER

Well, I don't know if sorry can make up for it. I found your
remarks highly offensive.

The CUSTOMER *stands silently, awaiting something.*

RANDAL
Well, if you think that's offensive . . .

RANDAL *flips open the magazine's centerfold—a graphic picture of a
woman with her vaginal lips and anus spread wide open.*

RANDAL

. . . then check this out. I think you can see her kidneys.

RANDAL *checks out the centerfold wistfully.* DANTE *frantically apologizes to the rapidly exiting* CUSTOMER.

DANTE

Ma'am, ma'am, I'm sorry! Please, wait a second, ma'am . . .

The CUSTOMER *is gone.* DANTE'S *pursuit stops at the counter.* DANTE *turns on* RANDAL.

DANTE

Why do you do things like that? You know she's going to come back and tell the boss.

RANDAL

Who cares? That lady's an asshole. Everybody that comes in here is way too uptight. This job would be great if it wasn't for the fucking customers.

DANTE

I'm gonna hear it tomorrow.

RANDAL

You gotta loosen up, my friend. You'd feel a hell of a lot better if you'd rip into the occasional customer.

DANTE

What for? They don't bother me if I don't bother them.

RANDAL

Liar! Tell me there aren't customers that annoy the piss out of you on a daily basis.

DANTE

There aren't.

RANDAL

How can you lie like that? Why don't you vent? Vent your frustration. Come on, who pisses you off?

                              DANTE
                           (reluctantly)
      It's not really anyone per se, it's more of separate groupings.

                              RANDAL
      Let's hear it.

                              DANTE
                             (pause)
      The milkmaids.

                              RANDAL
      The milkmaids?

INSERT: MILK HANDLER

*A WOMAN pulls out gallon after gallon, looking deep into the cooler for
that perfect container of milk.*

                           (OC) DANTE
      The women that go through every gallon of milk looking for a
      later date. As if somewhere—beyond all the other gallons—is a
      container of milk that won't go bad for like a decade.

END INSERT

                              RANDAL
      You know who I can do without? I could do without the people
      in the video store.

                              DANTE
      Which ones?

                              RANDAL
      All of them.

MONTAGE INSERT #1/VIDEO JERKS

A series of people addressing the camera, asking the dumb questions.

                              FIRST
      What would you get for a six-year-old boy who chronically wets
      his bed?

SECOND
(in front of stocked new release shelf)
Do you have any new movies in?

THIRD
Do you have that one with the guy who was in that movie that
was out last year?

END INSERT

RANDAL
And they never rent quality flicks; they always pick the most
intellectually devoid movie on the rack.

MONTAGE INSERT #2/"Ooooh! . . ."

An identical series of customers finding their ideal choices.

FIRST
Ooooh! *Home Alone*!

SECOND
Ooooh! *Hook*!

THIRD
Ooooh! *Navy Seals*!

END INSERT

RANDAL
It's like in order to join, they have to have an IQ less than their
shoe size.

DANTE
You think you get stupid questions? You should hear the barrage
of stupid questions I get.

MONTAGE INSERT #3/DUMB QUESTIONS

*A series of people standing in various locations throughout the
convenience store, asking truly dumb questions.*

FIRST
(holding coffee)
What do you mean there's no ice? You mean I've gotta drink this
coffee hot?!

SECOND
(holding up item from clearly marked $.99 display)
How much?

THIRD
(peeking in door)
Do you sell hubcaps?

END INSERT

RANDAL
See? You vented. Don't you feel better now?

DANTE
No.

RANDAL
Why not?

DANTE
Because my ex-girlfriend is getting married.

RANDAL
Jesus, you got a one-track mind. It's always
Caitlin, Caitlin, Caitlin . . .

DANTE
(jerking head toward door)
Veronica!

DANTE *gives* RANDAL *a shove to shut him up.* VERONICA *enters the
store, carrying books and something covered with aluminum foil.*

VERONICA
What happened to home by twelve?

DANTE *is suddenly by her side, taking the books from under her arm.*

DANTE

He still hasn't shown up. Why aren't you in class?

VERONICA

Lit 101 got canceled, so I stopped home and brought you some lunch.

DANTE

What is it?

VERONICA

Peanut butter and jelly with the crusts cut off. What do you think it is? It's lasagne.

DANTE

Really?
                    (kisses her forehead)
You're the best.

VERONICA

I'm glad you've calmed down a bit.
                    (to RANDAL)
Hi, Randal.

(OC) RANDAL
                    (exaggeratively impressed)
Thirty-seven!

DANTE
                    (to OC)
Shut up!
                    (to VERONICA)
Yes, I've calmed down. I'm still not happy about it, but I've been able to deal.

RANDAL *makes loud slurping noises from OC.*

DANTE
                    (to OC)
Why don't you go back to the video store?

RANDAL *walks past the two, and pats VERONICA on the head. He exits.*

VERONICA

You had to tell him.

DANTE

I had to tell someone. He put it into perspective.

VERONICA

What did he say?

DANTE

At least he wasn't thirty-six.

VERONICA

And that made you feel better?

DANTE

And he said most of them are college guys I've never met or seen.

VERONICA

The ostrich syndrome: if you don't see it . . .

DANTE

it isn't there. Yes.

VERONICA

Thank you for being rational.

DANTE

Thank you for the lasagne.

VERONICA

You couldn't get these shutters open?

DANTE

I called a locksmith and he said the earliest he could get here is tomorrow.

VERONICA

Bummer. Well, I've gotta head back for the one-thirty class.

DANTE

What time do you get finished?

VERONICA

Eight. But I have a sorority meeting till nine, so I'll be back before you close. Can we go out and get some coffee?

DANTE

Sure.

VERONICA

Good.

(kisses him)

I'll see you when you close, then. Enjoy the lasagne.

She exits. DANTE leans against the magazine rack with his lasagne, contemplative. RANDAL pops his head in and makes the loud slurping noise again. Cut to:

INT: VIDEO STORE. DAY

RANDAL is recommending titles to potential customers.

RANDAL

All right, now if you're really feeling dangerous tonight, then *Smokey and the Bandit Three* is the movie you must rent.

CUSTOMER

(studying box)

This doesn't even have Burt Reynolds in it.

RANDAL

Hey, neither did *ET*; but that was a great movie, right?

DANTE opens the door and leans in.

DANTE

Can you come next door? I gotta make a phone call.

RANDAL

(to DANTE)

Smokey Three: thumbs up, am I right?

DANTE

The best Burtless movie ever made.

DANTE exits. RANDAL gives his customers the what-did-I-tell-you look. Cut to:

INT: CONVENIENCE STORE. DAY

THE CAT *lies on the counter. Pull back to reveal* RANDAL *as he rings up an order. The* CUSTOMER *pets the cat, smiling.*

CUSTOMER

Awww, he's so cute. What's his name?

RANDAL

Lenin's Tomb.

Dolly over to DANTE, *on the phone.*

DANTE

Hello, is Mr. Snyder there? This is Dante . . . Did he say if he was on his way here? . . . Here . . . The convenience store . . . I know, but the other guy called out this morning and Mr. Snyder asked me to cover until he got here. He said he'd be here by noon, but it's one-thirty now, so I . . . Excuse me . . . Vermont!? . . . No, that can't be; I talked to him this morning . . . He left at what time? . . . He really went to Vermont? . . . When the hell was someone going to tell me? . . . He promised he was coming by noon! . . . Jesus . . . When does he get back?! . . . TUESDAY! . . . You've gotta be fucking kidding me! . . . I've got a hockey game at two, and the fucking shutters are jammed closed, and he's in Vermont? . . . I'm not even supposed to be here today!!
(deep sigh)
So I'm stuck here till closing? . . . This is just great . . . I just can't believe . . . I'm sorry, I didn't mean to yell at you . . . No . . . No, I'll be all right . . . Well, that's all I can do, right? . . . Thanks.

He hangs up. RANDAL *joins him.*

RANDAL

Vermont?

DANTE

Can you believe this?!

RANDAL

He didn't mention it when he called you this morning?

DANTE

Not a fucking word! Slippery shit!

RANDAL

So, what—you're stuck here all day?

DANTE

FUCK!

RANDAL

Why'd you apologize?

DANTE

What?

RANDAL

I heard you apologize. Why? You have every right in the world to be mad.

DANTE

I know.

RANDAL

That seems to be the leitmotif in your life; ever backing down.

DANTE

I don't back down.

RANDAL

Yes, you do. You always back down. You assume blame that isn't yours, you come in when called as opposed to enjoying your day off, you buckle like a belt.

DANTE

You know what pisses me off the most?

RANDAL

The fact that I'm right about your buckling?

DANTE

I'm going to miss the game.

RANDAL

Because you buckled.

DANTE
Would you shut the hell up with that shit? It's not helping.

RANDAL
Don't yell at me, pal.

DANTE
Sorry.

RANDAL
See? There you go again.

DANTE
I can't believe I'm going to miss the game!

RANDAL
At least we're stuck here together.

DANTE
You've got a customer.

RANDAL *walks away.*

(OC) RANDAL
What? What do you want?!

DANTE *shakes his head in frustration and picks up the phone again.*

DANTE
Sanford? Dante . . . I can't play today . . . I'm stuck at work . . . I
know I'm not scheduled, but—just forget it. I can't play . . .
Neither can Randal. . . . He's working too. . . .

RANDAL *comes back.* DANTE *rolls his eyes to the ceiling.*

DANTE
(getting an idea)
Wait a second. Do we have to play at the park? . . . Hold on . . .
(to RANDAL*)*
Do you feel limber?

Cut to:

INT: CONVENIENCE STORE. DAY

*TAPE is rolled around the top of a stick. Laces are pulled tightly. An
orange ball is slapped back and forth by a blade. The* HOCKEY
PLAYERS *fill the convenience store. Some sit on the floor or lean against
the coolers, but all are either preparing or practicing.* RANDAL *enters,
wearing his equipment.* DANTE *skates to his side.*

> DANTE
> *(lifting his foot)*
> Pull my laces tighter.

> RANDAL
> *(drops mitt and pulls laces)*
> I've gotta tell you, my friend: this is one of the ballsiest moves
> I've ever been privy to. I never would have thought you capable
> of such blatant disregard of store policy.

> DANTE
> I told him I had a game today. It's his own fault.

> RANDAL
> No argument here. Insubordination rules.

> DANTE
> I just want to play hockey like I was scheduled to.

SANFORD *skates up and skids to a halt.*

> SANFORD
> Dante, let me grab a Gatorade.

> DANTE
> If you grab a Gatorade, then everyone's going to grab one.

> SANFORD
> So?

> DANTE
> So? So nobody's going to want to pay for these Gatorades.

SANFORD

What do you care? Hey, what smells like shoe polish?

DANTE

I've got a responsibility here. I can't let everybody grab free drinks.

SANFORD

What responsibility? You're closing the fucking store to play hockey.

RANDAL

He's blunt, but he's got a point.

DANTE

At least let me maintain some semblance of managerial control here.

SANFORD

All I'm saying is if you're going to be insubordinate, you should go the full nine and not pussy out when it comes to free refreshments.

RANDAL

He's right. As if we're suddenly gonna have a run on Gatorade.

SANFORD

Fuckin-A.

DANTE

All right. Jesus, you fuckers are pushy.

SANFORD

Hey man, I hear Caitlin's marrying an Asian drum major.

RANDAL

Design major.

DANTE

Can we not talk about this?

                              SANFORD
          Fine by me. But you're living in denial and suppressing rage.
                          (skating away; to all)
          Dante said we can all drink free Gatorade.

A laid-back hurrah is heard.

                              RANDAL
          Are you gonna lock the store?

                              DANTE
          I don't know. You going to lock the video store?

                              RANDAL
          Look who you're asking here. How're we gonna block off the
          street?

                              DANTE
          We're not playing in the street.

                              RANDAL
          Then where're we gonna play?

Cut to:

EXT: CONVENIENCE STORE. DAY

The sign on the door reads:

TEMPORARILY CLOSED. BE OPENED AFTER FIRST PERIOD.

*The PLAYERS ascend a ladder adjacent to the door, one by one. ON THE
ROOF they jump off the ladder and skate around. More players join them.
From across the street we get the full, odd perspective: a store with many
men gliding around on the roof.*

*On the roof DANTE skates and passes with another player. REDDING
stretches, leaning against the sign. RANDAL pulls his mask on and slaps
his glove, urging a shot. SANFORD skates in and takes a shot, which
RANDAL blocks. JAY and SILENT BOB deal to a player: he drops
money over the ledge and JAY throws up a dime bag. DANTE holds a
ball in the center of the court.*

DANTE
Ready?

PLAYERS *take positions. SANFORD comes to the center and holds the ball in drop position. DANTE and REDDING face off, and the ball is in play.*

The game begins as the players engage in a savage ballet. Faces are smashed with sticks, slide tackles are made, shots are taken, CU's of various players included.

INACTIVE PLAYERS *call out encouragement and slander from the sidelines. More game playing including both goalies getting scored on and more face-offs.*

Below, a CUSTOMER *tugs on the convenience store door. He reads the sign and then backs up into the street, attempting to peer over the ledge. Above, the game continues.*

Below, the CUSTOMER *shifts from one foot to the other impatiently. He grabs the ladder and quickly ascends.*

Above, from over the ledge of the roof, we see the head of the customer peek. Skating feet pass rapidly before him, and he watches for a moment before calling out.

CUSTOMER
When's this period over?

SOMEONE O.C.
Eight more minutes!

CUSTOMER
Are you shitting me? I want to get cigarettes!

DANTE *skids to the sidelines.*

DANTE
(out of breath)
If you can just wait a few more minutes.

CUSTOMER
Fuck that! I'm gonna break my crazy neck on this ladder!

                    (OC) SOMEONE
          Dante! Where are you?!

                    CUSTOMER
          He's busy!

DANTE *starts to skate away.*

                    DANTE
          I'll be right back. It's almost over.

He jumps back into the game.

                    CUSTOMER
          What the fuck is this?! I want some service!

                    (OC) DANTE
          In a second!

                    CUSTOMER
          Fuck in a second! This is . . . Look at you! You can't even pass!

                    (OC) DANTE
          I can pass!

                    CUSTOMER
          How 'bout covering point!? You suck!

DANTE *skids back to the sidelines to address the* CUSTOMER.

                    DANTE
          Who are you to make assessments?

                    CUSTOMER
          I'll assess all I want!

                    (OC) SOMEONE
          DANTE! ARE YOU IN OR OUT!

                    CUSTOMER
                    (to O.C. SOMEONE)
          Don't pass to this guy! He sucks!
                    (to DANTE)
          You suck!

DANTE

Like you're better!

CUSTOMER

I can whip your ass.

Below, a WOMAN pulls at the door. She peers into the store, face against the glass.

(OC) DANTE

That's easy to say from over here.

(OC) CUSTOMER

Give me a stick, pretty boy! I'll knock your fucking teeth out and pass all over your ass.

The WOMAN backs up and, shielding her eyes, looks toward the roof.

WOMAN

Is the convenience store open?

Above, DANTE and the CUSTOMER shout down at the OC WOMAN.

DANTE AND CUSTOMER
(simultaneously)

NO!

DANTE
(to CUSTOMER)

There's a stick over there. You're shooting against the goal.
(to the court)
REDDING! COME OFF AND LET THIS FUCK ON!

A new face-off pits DANTE against the CUSTOMER. The ball drops between the two and DANTE gets flattened. The CUSTOMER winds up and takes a hard shot. The ball sails off the court, through the air, and into a faraway yard. DANTE calls to the sidelines.

DANTE

Give me another ball.

(OC) SOMEONE

There are no more.

What the fuck are you talking about? How many balls did you
bring?

SANFORD *skates up to him.*

SANFORD
(counting)
There was the orange ball . . . and the orange ball.

DANTE *scrambles to the ledge and calls over.*

DANTE
Are there any balls down there?!

(OC) JAY
'Bout the biggest pair you ever seen! NYNNE!!

DANTE *looks around, hyperventilating.*

DANTE
You only brought one ball?!

SANFORD
I thought Redding had like three balls!

(OC) REDDING
I thought Dante had the balls.

DANTE
Nobody has another ball?

SANFORD
Shit!

DANTE
We get . . . what . . . twelve minutes of game, and it's over? Fuck!
Fuck! Fuck! Fuck!!
(pause; rubs head)
I'm not even supposed to be here today!

DANTE *skates off.*

SANFORD
We still get free Gatorade, right?

CUT TO:

INT: CONVENIENCE STORE. DAY

DANTE *standing on a ladder, replaces a fluorescent light. An* OLD MAN *joins him at the foot of the ladder.*

OLD MAN
Be careful.

DANTE
I'm trying.

OLD MAN
You know the insides of those are filled with stuff that gives you cancer.

DANTE
So I'm told.

OLD MAN
I had a friend that used to chew glass for a living. In the circus.

The light in place, DANTE *descends the ladder and closes it.*

DANTE
And he got cancer by chewing fluorescent bulb glass . . . ?

OLD MAN
No, he got hit by a bus.

DANTE
(confused)
Oh . . . Can I help you?

OLD MAN
Well, that depends. Do you have a bathroom?

DANTE
Um . . . yeah, but it's for employees only.

OLD MAN

I understand, but can I use it. I'm not that young anymore, so I'm kind of . . . you know . . . incontinent.

DANTE

Uh . . . sure. Go ahead. It's back through the cooler.

OLD MAN

Thanks son. Say—what kind of toilet paper you got back there?

DANTE

The white kind.

OLD MAN

I'm not asking about the color. I mean is it rough or cottony?

DANTE

Actually, it is kind of rough.

OLD MAN

Rough, eh? Oh, that stuff rips hell out of my hemorrhoids. Say, would you mind if I took a roll of the soft stuff back there. I see you sell the soft stuff.

DANTE

Yeah, but . . .

OLD MAN

Aw, c'mon boy. What's the difference? You said yourself the stuff that's there now is rough.

DANTE

Yeah, okay. Go ahead.

OLD MAN

Thanks son, you're a lifesaver.

The OLD MAN *walks off.* DANTE *heads back to the counter. The* OLD MAN *returns.*

OLD MAN

Say, young fella; you know I hate to bother you again, but can I take a paper or something back there . . . to read? It usually takes me a while, and I like to read while it's going on.

DANTE

Jesus . . . go ahead.

OLD MAN

Thanks, young man. You've got a heart of gold.

The OLD MAN sifts through some papers and a few magazines. He comes back to the counter.

DANTE

You know, you probably could've been home, already, in the time it's taken you to get in there.

OLD MAN

Can I trouble you for one of those magazines?

DANTE

I said go ahead.

OLD MAN

No, I mean the ones there. Behind the counter.

DANTE *glances over and reacts.*

DANTE

The porno mags?

OLD MAN

Yeah. I like the cartoons. They make me laugh. They draw the biggest titties.

DANTE
(hands one to him)
Here. Now leave me alone.

OLD MAN

Uh, can I have the other one. The one below this one. They show more in that one.

DANTE *makes the switch.*

OLD MAN

Thanks son. I appreciate this.

The OLD MAN *walks off. We hear the back door open and close, then the
front door does the same.* RANDAL *joins* DANTE.

RANDAL

Helluva game!

DANTE

One ball!! They come all the way here . . . I close the damn store
. . . for one ball!

RANDAL

Hockey's hockey. At least we got to play.

DANTE

Randal, twelve minutes is not a game! Jesus, it's barely a warm-
up!

RANDAL

Bitch, bitch, bitch. You want something to drink?
(walking away)

DANTE

Gatorade.

Pause. Then . . .

(OC) RANDAL

What happened to all the Gatorade?

DANTE

Exactly. They drank it all.

(OC) RANDAL

After an exhausting game like that I can believe it.

DANTE
(as RANDAL*)*

"It's not like we're gonna sell out."

RANDAL *comes back with drinks.*

RANDAL
You know what Sanford told me?
(offering drink)

DANTE
I still can't believe Caitlin's getting married.

RANDAL
Julie Dwyer died.

DANTE
Yeah, right.

RANDAL
No, I'm serious.

DANTE *is visibly taken aback.*

DANTE
Oh, my god.

RANDAL
Sanford's brother dates her cousin. He found out this morning.

DANTE
How? When?

RANDAL
Embolism in her brain. Yesterday.

DANTE
Jesus.

RANDAL
She was swimming at the YMCA pool when it happened. Died midbackstroke.

DANTE
I haven't seen her in almost two years.

RANDAL
Correct me if I'm wrong, but wasn't she one of the illustrious twelve?

DANTE

Number six.

RANDAL

You've had sex with a dead person.

DANTE

I'm gonna go to her wake.

RANDAL

No, you're not.

DANTE

Why not?

RANDAL

It's today.

DANTE

What!?

RANDAL

Paulsen's Funeral Parlor. The next show is at four.

DANTE

Shit. What about tomorrow?

RANDAL

One night only. She's buried in the morning.

DANTE

You've gotta watch the store. I have to go to this.

RANDAL

Wait, wait, wait. Has it occurred to you that I might be bereaved
as well?

DANTE

You hardly knew her!

RANDAL

True, but do you know how many people are going to be there?
All of our old classmates, to say the least.

DANTE

Stop it. This is beneath even you.

RANDAL

I'm not missing what's probably going to be the social event of
the season.

DANTE

You hate people.

RANDAL

But I love gatherings. Isn't it ironic?

DANTE

Don't be an asshole. Somebody has to stay with the store.

RANDAL

If you go, I go.

DANTE

She meant nothing to you!

RANDAL

She meant nothing to you either until I told you she died.

DANTE

I'm not taking you to this funeral.

RANDAL

I'm going with you.

DANTE

I can't close the store.

RANDAL

You just closed the store to play hockey on the roof!

DANTE

Exactly, which means I can't close it for another hour so we can
both go to a wake.

Cut to:

INT CAR: DAY

DANTE *drives with passenger* RANDAL, their backs to the camera.

> RANDAL
> You were saying?

> DANTE
> Thanks for putting me in a tough spot. You're a good friend.

Silence. Then . . .

> RANDAL
> She was pretty young, hunhh?

> DANTE
> Twenty-two; same as us.

> RANDAL
> An embolism in a pool.

> DANTE
> An embarrassing way to die.

> RANDAL
> That's nothing compared to how my cousin Walter died.

> DANTE
> How'd he die?

> RANDAL
> Broke his neck.

> DANTE
> That's embarrassing?

> RANDAL
> He broke his neck trying to suck his own dick.

Absolute silence. Then . . .

DANTE

Shut the hell up.

RANDAL

Bible truth.

DANTE

Stop it.

RANDAL

I swear.

DANTE

Oh, my god.

RANDAL

Come on. Haven't you ever tried to suck your own dick?

DANTE

No!

RANDAL

Yeah sure. You're so repressed.

DANTE

Because I never tried to suck my own dick?

RANDAL

No, because you won't admit to it. As if a guy's a fucking pervert
because he tries to go down on himself. You're as curious as the
rest of us, pal. You've tried it.

DANTE

Who found him?

RANDAL

My cousin? My aunt found him. On his bed, doubled over himself
with his legs on top. Dick in his mouth. My aunt freaked out. It
was a mess.

DANTE

His dick was in his mouth?

                         RANDAL
Balls resting on his lips.

                         DANTE
He made it, hunhh?

                         RANDAL
Yeah, but at what a price.

Silence. Then . . .

                         DANTE
I could never reach.

                         RANDAL
Reach what?

                         DANTE
You know.

                         RANDAL
What, your dick?

                         DANTE
Yeah. Like you said, you know. I guess everyone tries it, sooner
or later.

                         RANDAL
I never tried it.

DANTE *glares at* RANDAL. *Silence. Then . . .*

Fucking pervert.

Cut to:

EXT: FUNERAL PARLOR. DAY

DANTE *and* RANDAL *walk up the path to the funeral parlor.*

                         DANTE
I know it was a bad idea to close the store.

RANDAL.
Listen to you.

DANTE
I can't help it. At least when we were playing hockey outside, I could see if anyone wanted to go in.

RANDAL
Nobody's there. It's four o'clock on a Saturday. How many people ever come to the store at four on a Saturday?

Cut to:

EXT: CONVENIENCE STORE. DAY

A MASSIVE CROWD *is outside the store. Cut to:*

EXT: FUNERAL PARLOR. DAY

DANTE *and* RANDAL *run from the front door, closely chased by a small crowd of angry mourners. Car locks are slammed down. The car screams away. The pursuing crowd stands in the middle of the street, shaking their fists, throwing things. Cut to:*

EXT: CONVENIENCE STORE. NIGHT

The car pulls up and RANDAL *and* DANTE *get out. Absolutely nobody is outside.*

DANTE
(furious)
I can't fucking believe you!!

RANDAL
I'm telling you, it wasn't my fault!

DANTE
You knocked the fucking casket over, for Chrissakes!

RANDAL
I was just leaning on it! It was an accident!

DANTE
Does anyone ever knock over a casket on purpose?

RANDAL
So the casket fell over! Big deal!

DANTE
Her fucking body fell out!

RANDAL
So they'll put her back in! It's not like it's gonna matter if she breaks something!

DANTE
(opening door)
Just . . . go! Go open the video store.

(OC) JAY
(mimicking)
Yeah! Open the video store!!

RANDAL
(to OC)
Shut the fuck up, junkie!

JAY *enters the frame, right next to* RANDAL. *He aims his butt at him and farts.* RANDAL *lunges for him.* DANTE *grabs* RANDAL.

DANTE
(to RANDAL)
Go open the video store.

JAY
Yeah, you cock-smoking clerk.

DANTE
(to JAY)
How many times I gotta tell you not to deal outside the store.

JAY
I'm not dealing.

A KID *tugs at* JAY'S *shirt.*

KID
You got anything, man?

>   JAY
>   Yeah, what do you want?

RANDAL *heads to the video store.* DANTE *enters the convenience store and slides the sign to* OPEN. *After a few seconds, the* IMPATIENT CUSTOMER *(guy who lost his keys) appears, flashlight in hand, scanning the ground.*

>   IMPATIENT CUSTOMER
>   *(to* JAY*)*
>   Hey, did you see a set of keys lying around here somewhere?

Cut to:

INT: CONVENIENCE STORE. NIGHT

DANTE *rearranges the milk.* RANDAL *joins him.*

>   RANDAL
>   Let me borrow your car.

>   DANTE
>   I don't want to talk to you.

>   RANDAL
>   Fine. Just lend me your car.

>   DANTE
>   Why should I loan you my car?

>   RANDAL
>   I want to rent a movie.

>   DANTE
>   *(pause)*
>   You want to rent a movie.

>   RANDAL
>   I want to rent a movie.

DANTE *walks away, shaking his head.*

>   RANDAL
>   What's that for?

You work in a video store!

They head back to the counter.

RANDAL

I work in a shitty video store. I want to go to a good video store
so I can rent a good movie.

CUSTOMER

Are you open?

DANTE *and* RANDAL
(simultaneously)

YES!

The CUSTOMER *comes to the counter.*

CUSTOMER

Pack of cigarettes.
(pets cat)
Cute cat. What's its name?

RANDAL

Annoying Customer.

The CUSTOMER *lets it sink in, and then leaves in a huff.* DANTE *puts
up cigarettes.*

DANTE

Can you imagine being halfway decent to the customers at least
some of the time?

RANDAL

Let me borrow your car.

DANTE
(calmer)

May I be blunt with you? ´

RANDAL

If you must.

DANTE
We are employees of Quick Stop Convenience and RST video, respectively. As such, we have certain responsibilities which—though it may seem cruel and unusual—does include manning our posts until closing.

RANDAL
I see. So playing hockey and attending wakes—these practices are standard operating procedure.

DANTE
There's a difference. Those were obligations. Obligations that could not have been met at any later date. Now renting videos—that's just gratuitous, not to mention illogical, considering you work in a video store.

Another CUSTOMER *leans in.*

CUSTOMER
Are you open?

DANTE
(rolls his eyes)
Yes.

RANDAL
You know what? I don't think I care for your rationale.

DANTE
It's going to have to do for now, considering that it's my car that's up for request.

(to CUSTOMER*)*

Can I help you?

CUSTOMER
Pack of cigarettes.

RANDAL
What's your point?

DANTE

My point is that you're a clerk, paid to do a job. You can't just do anything you want while you're working.

CUSTOMER
(reading tabloid)

"Space Alien Revealed as Head of Time Warner; Reports Stock Increase."

(to DANTE and RANDAL)

They print any kind of shit in these papers.

DANTE

They certainly do. Two fifty-five.

RANDAL

So your argument is that title dictates behavior?

DANTE

What?

RANDAL

The reason you won't let me borrow your car is because I have a title and a job description, and I'm supposed to follow it, right?

DANTE

Exactly.

CUSTOMER
(interjecting)

I saw one, one time, that said the world was ending the next week. Then in the next week's paper, they said we were miraculously saved at the zero hour by a Koala-fish mutant bird. Crazy shit.

RANDAL
(eyes the CUSTOMER, annoyed)

So I'm no more responsible for my own decisions while I'm here at work than, say, the Death Squad soldiers in Bosnia?

DANTE

That's stretching it. You're not being asked to slay children or anything.

Not yet.

(sips water)

CUSTOMER
(again with the interjections)
And I remember this one time the damn paper said . . .

RANDAL *spits a mist of water at the customer, drenching him. The man reacts violently, attempting to grab* RANDAL *from over the counter.* RANDAL *makes no move, but remains untouched.* DANTE *plays block.*

CUSTOMER
I'M GONNA BREAK YOUR FUCKING HEAD! YOU FUCKING JERKOFF!

DANTE
Sir! Sir, I'm sorry! He didn't mean it! He was trying to get me.

CUSTOMER
Well, he missed!

DANTE
I know. I'm sorry. Let me refund your cigarette money, and we'll call it even.

CUSTOMER
(considerably calmer; takes money)
This is the last time I ever come here.
(to RANDAL*)*
And if I ever see you again, I'm gonna break your fucking head open!

The CUSTOMER *leaves, wiping water from his face.* RANDAL *salutes him.*

DANTE
(angrily)
What the fuck did you do that for?

RANDAL
Two reasons: one, I hate when the people can't shut up about the stupid tabloid headlines.

DANTE

Jesus!

RANDAL

And two, to make a point: title does not dictate behavior.

DANTE

What?

RANDAL

If title dictated my behavior, as a clerk serving the public, I wouldn't be allowed to spit a mouthful of water at that guy. But I did, so my point is that people dictate their own behavior. Hence, even though I'm a clerk in this video store, I choose to go rent videos at Big Choice.
                    (extends opened palm)
Agreed?

DANTE
        (shakes his head; hands over keys)
You're a danger to both the dead and the living.

RANDAL

I like to think I'm a master of my own destiny.

DANTE

Please, get the hell out of here.

RANDAL

I know I'm your hero.

RANDAL *exits. Cut to:*

INT: CONVENIENCE STORE. DAY

DANTE *waits on a customer (*TRAINER*). He lifts the gallon of milk into a paper bag, letting out a slight grunt.*

TRAINER

Sounds to me like somebody needs to hit the gym.

DANTE

Excuse me?

TRAINER

I heard you strain when you put the milk in the bag. That milk
only weighs about seven pounds.

DANTE

I didn't strain. I sighed.

TRAINER

I don't think so. That was a grunt; a deep inhalation of oxygen to
aid in the stretching of muscles. I'm a trainer. I know what that
sound signifies: you're out of shape.

DANTE

I don't think so.

TRAINER

Oh, I do. You made the same noise when you reached across the
counter for my cash. Your muscles are thin and sadly
underutilized.

DANTE

They are not.

TRAINER

Yes, they are. You're out of shape.

DANTE

What are you talking about? There's no fat on this body.

TRAINER

No fat, but no tone either. You don't get enough exercise.

A female customer (HEATHER) leans in the doorway.

HEATHER

Are you open?

DANTE

Yes.

HEATHER
(grabs a paper)

Just the paper.

DANTE
(to HEATHER*)*

Thirty-five.

TRAINER
(to HEATHER*)*

Let me ask you a question: Do you think this guy's out of shape?

HEATHER
(studies DANTE*)*

I don't know. I can't really tell from here.

TRAINER

He is.

DANTE

I am not.

TRAINER

How much can you bench?

DANTE

I don't know.

HEATHER
(studying DANTE*)*

I'd say about sixty, seventy—tops.

DANTE

I know I can bench more than that!

TRAINER

I think the lady called it.

HEATHER

My ex-boyfriend was about his height, but he was much bulkier.
He could bench two-fifty, three hundred easy.

TRAINER

I do about three-fifty, four.

HEATHER

No way!

                    TRAINER
                (rolling up sleeve)
Feel that.

                    HEATHER
That's tight. Solid.

                    TRAINER
Now feel his.
                    (to DANTE*)*
Roll up your sleeve, chief.

                    DANTE
Oh for God's sake!

                    TRAINER
See? You're ashamed. You know you're out of shape. Take my
card. I can help you tone that body up in no time. Get you on an
aerobics and free-weights program.

A SUITED MAN *carrying a notebook comes to the counter.*

                    SUITED MAN
You open?

                    DANTE
                (to MAN*)*
Yes.
                (to TRAINER*)*
I'm not out of shape.

                    SUITED MAN
Excuse me, but have you been here all day?

                    DANTE
What?

                    HEATHER
            (still studying DANTE*)*
He's got those love handles.

                    DANTE
                (to HEATHER*)*
I don't have love handles.

SUITED MAN

Were you working here at about four o'clock?

DANTE

I've been here since six o'clock this morning. Why?

TRAINER
(to HEATHER*)*

It's probably from being around all this food every day.

HEATHER

Oh, I know. If I had to work here all day, I'd be bloated and out of shape, too.

DANTE

I'm not out of shape!

SUITED MAN

Can I have your name please?

DANTE

Dante Hicks. Why? What is this about?

The SUITED MAN *scribbles in his notebook.*

HEATHER

You're Dante Hicks? Oh my God! I didn't even recognize you!

TRAINER

Because he's out of shape.

DANTE

Do I know you?

HEATHER

Do you remember Alyssa Jones? She hung out with . . .

DANTE

Caitlin Bree. Yeah?

HEATHER

I'm her sister.

DANTE

You're Alyssa's sister? Heather?

HEATHER

Yep. I remember you got caught in my parents' room with Caitlin once.

TRAINER

Did you say Caitlin Bree?

DANTE

Yeah.

TRAINER

Pretty girl, about this girl's height—dark hair—gorgeous body?

DANTE

Yeah?

TRAINER

And your name is Dante Hicks? You went to high school with her? You played hockey?

DANTE

How do you know that?

TRAINER

Oh man! Hey, you still going out with her?

DANTE

No, she's getting married.

TRAINER

To you?

HEATHER

To an Asian design major.

TRAINER

Shit!
                    (to DANTE*)*
Don't take this the wrong way, but I used to fuck her.

DANTE
What?

TRAINER
While you two were dating in high school. We're talking four,
five years ago, back when I drove a Trans-Am.

HEATHER
Oh my God! You're Rick Derris?

TRAINER
Yeah!

DANTE
You know him?

HEATHER
Caitlin used to talk about him all the time.

TRAINER
Really?

HEATHER
Oh yeah. You were the built older guy with the black Trans and
the big . . .

DANTE
Wait a second!
(to TRAINER)
You used to sleep with Caitlin Bree? While I was dating her?

TRAINER
All the time. That girl was like a rabbit.

DANTE
I . . . I don't believe this. . . .

HEATHER
(to TRAINER)
I still remember Caitlin telling us about that time you two went to
that motel—the one with the mirrors and the hot tub in the room.

DANTE
THE GLADES MOTEL?

TRAINER

Holy shit! She told you about that!

(to DANTE)

Buddy of mine worked there. Said he watched the whole thing.
They used to film people at that hotel; nobody knew about it.

HEATHER

She said one time you set up a tent on the beach and you guys
did it in the middle of this big rainstorm.

DANTE

What? When? When did all this shit happen?

TRAINER

Hey man, that was a long time ago. Don't let it get to you.

HEATHER

I'm surprised you never found out about it, Dante. Everybody in
school knew—even in my class.

DANTE

Jesus Christ, what next?

The SUITED MAN *rips a piece of paper out of his notebook and hands it
to* DANTE.

SUITED MAN

Here you go.

DANTE

What's this?

SUITED MAN

A fine, for five hundred dollars.

DANTE

WHAT?

TRAINER

Five hundred bucks? What for?

SUITED MAN

For violation of New Jersey Statute Section Two A, number one-
seventy slash fifty-one: Any person who sells or makes available

tobacco or tobacco-related products to persons under the age of eighteen is regarded as disorderly.

DANTE

What are you talking about?

SUITED MAN

According to the NJAC—the New Jersey Administrative Code, section eighteen, five, slash twelve point five—a fine of no less than two hundred and fifty dollars is to be leveled against any person reported selling cigarettes to a minor.

DANTE

I didn't do that!

SUITED MAN

You said you were here all day?

DANTE

Yeah, but I didn't sell cigarettes to any kids!

SUITED MAN

An angry mother called the state division of taxation and complained that the man working at Quick Stop Convenience sold her five-year-old daughter cigarettes today at around four o'clock. Division of taxation calls the State Board of Health, and they send me down here to issue a fine. You say you were working all day, hence the fine is yours. It's doubled due to the incredibly young age of the child.

DANTE

But I didn't sell cigarettes to any kid!

TRAINER

To a five-year-old kid? What a scumbag!

HEATHER

That's sick, Dante.

DANTE

I didn't sell cigarettes to any kids! I swear!

SUITED MAN

The due date is on the bottom. This summons cannot be contested
in any court of law. Failure to remit before the due date will result
in a charge of criminal negligence, and a warrant will be issued
for your arrest. Have a nice day.

The SUITED MAN *exits, with* DANTE *trying to follow.*

DANTE

But I didn't sell cigarettes to any kids! Hey!

TRAINER
(takes back the card)
Forget it. I don't want to deal with a guy that sells cigarettes to a
five-year-old.
(to HEATHER*)*
Can I offer you a ride somewhere?

HEATHER

Sure. How about the beach?

TRAINER

I like the way you think.

The two exit. DANTE, *alone, studies his summons. He rubs his forehead.*

DANTE

Jesus! What next?

(OC) VOICE

Dante?

DANTE *spins, angrily.*

DANTE

What?

His expression softens.

Caitlin?

Cut to:

EXT: VIDEO STORE. NIGHT

JAY *deals with a customer as* SILENT BOB *looks on.*

> JAY
>
> That's the price, my brother.

> JOHN
>
> Yo, I don't have that kind of cash.

> JAY
>
> For this kind of hash, you need that kind of cash.

> JOHN
>
> How long you gonna be here?

> JAY
>
> Till ten. Then I'm going to John K's party.

> JOHN
>
> You're gonna be at John K's party?

> JAY
> *(to* SILENT BOB)
>
> My man is deaf.
> *(yelling)*
> I'M GOING TO JOHN K'S PARTY!
> *(quieter)*
> Neh.

> JOHN
>
> Yo, don't sell all that. 'Cause I'm gonna get the cash and buy it from you at John K's. You're gonna bring it, right?

> JAY
>
> The only place I don't bring my drugs is church. And that ain't till Sunday morning.

> JOHN
>
> Yo. I'll see you at that party.
> *(puts his hand up to be slapped)*
> I'll see you there?

JAY
(reluctantly slapping hands)
I'll see you there.

JOHN *leaves.* JAY *turns to* SILENT BOB.

JAY
It's motherfuckers like that who give recreational drug users a
bad name.
(suddenly spotting someone OC)
HEY BABY! YOU EVER HAD YOUR ASSHOLE LICKED?

Cut to:

INT: CONVENIENCE STORE. NIGHT

DANTE *and* CAITLIN *are embracing very tightly. We hold on them for a
few seconds, just to let it sink in. Then . . .*

DANTE
When did you get back?

CAITLIN
Just now.

DANTE
My God. I haven't seen you since . . .
(he hugs her again)

CAITLIN
Dante. You've got a customer.

DANTE *hops behind the counter. A customer pays for something while*
DANTE *continues to talk.*

CAITLIN
I just saw Alyssa's little sister outside. She was with Rick Derris.

DANTE
Let's not talk about that. How'd you get home?

CAITLIN
Train. It took eight hours.

                              DANTE
        I can't believe you're here.

Another customer comes to the counter.

                            CUSTOMER
        Excuse me, do you have . . .

                              DANTE
                          (to CUSTOMER*)*
        To the back, above the oil.
                          (to CAITLIN*)*
        How long are you staying?

                            CAITLIN
        Until Monday. Then I have to take the train back.

Yet another customer comes to the counter.

                            CUSTOMER
        Pack of cigarettes.
                          (to CAITLIN*)*
        Congratulations. I saw that announcement in today's paper.
                          (to DANTE*)*
        She's marrying an Asian design major.

                              DANTE
        So I'm told.

Cut to:

EXT: VIDEO STORE. NIGHT

JAY *and* SILENT BOB *lean against the wall.*

                               JAY
        Man, it's fucking slow.

SILENT BOB *walks out of the frame, leaving* JAY *alone against the wall.
He comes back a few seconds later, carrying a mini-Walkman with ten-
watt speakers. He sets it down on the ground and turns it on. House music
starts playing. Jay—possessed by the beat—breaks into an impromptu*

dance, in which he makes suggestive and often lewd moves. SILENT BOB
leans against the wall. Cut to:

INT: VIDEO STORE. NIGHT

On counter

> CAITLIN
>
> You're just going to lock the store like that?

> DANTE
>
> I want to talk to you about something, and I don't want to be
> disturbed.

> CAITLIN
>
> You saw it?

> DANTE
>
> Very dramatic, I thought.

> CAITLIN
>
> It's not what you think.

> DANTE
>
> What, it's worse? You're pregnant with an Asian design major's
> child?

> CAITLIN
>
> I'm not pregnant.

> DANTE
>
> Were you going to tell me or just send me an invitation?

> CAITLIN
>
> I was going to tell you. But then we were getting along so well, I
> didn't want to mess it up.

> DANTE
>
> You could've broke it to me gently, you know; at least started by
> telling me you had a boyfriend. I told you I had a girlfriend.

> CAITLIN
>
> I know, I'm sorry. But when we started talking . . . it's like I
> forgot I had a boyfriend. And then he proposed last month. . . .

DANTE

And you said yes?

CAITLIN

Well . . . kind of, sort of?

DANTE

Is that what they teach you at that school of yours? Kind of, sort of? Everyone knows about this except me! Do you know how humiliating that is?

CAITLIN

I would've told you, and you would have stopped calling, like a baby.

DANTE

How do you know that?

CAITLIN

Because I know you. You prefer drastic measures to rational ones.

DANTE

So you're really getting married?

CAITLIN

No.

DANTE

No, you're not really getting married?

CAITLIN

The story goes like this: He proposed, and I told him I had to think about it, and he insisted I wear the ring anyway. Then my mother told the paper we were engaged.

DANTE

How like her.

CAITLIN

Then my mother called me this morning and told me the announcement was in the paper. That's when I hopped the train to come back here, because I knew you'd be a wreck.

DANTE

Thanks for the vote of confidence.

CAITLIN

Was I right?

DANTE

Wreck is a harsh term. Disturbed is more like it. Mildly disturbed
even.

CAITLIN

I love a macho facade. It's such a turn-on.
(sniffing air)
What smells like shoe polish?

DANTE

And you came here to what? To comfort me?

CAITLIN

The last thing I needed was for you to think I was hiding
something from you.

DANTE

But you were.

CAITLIN

No, I wasn't. Not really. I told you'd I'd been seeing other people.

DANTE

Yeah, but not seriously. Christ, you're ready to walk down the
aisle—I'd say that constitutes something more than just seeing
somebody.

CAITLIN

I'm giving him his ring back.

DANTE

What?

CAITLIN

I don't want to marry him. I don't want to get married now. I'm
on the verge of graduation. I want to go to grad school after this.
And then I want to start a career. I don't want to be a wife first,

and then have to worry about when I'm going to fit in all of the other stuff. I've come way too far and studied too hard to let my education go to waste as a housewife. And I know that's what I'd become. Sang's already signed with a major firm, and he's going to be pulling a huge salary, which would give me no reason to work, and he's so traditional anyway . . .

DANTE

Sang? His name is a past tense?

CAITLIN

Stop it. He's a nice guy.

DANTE

If he's so nice, why aren't you going to marry him?

CAITLIN

I just told you.

DANTE

There's more, isn't there?

CAITLIN

Why, Mr. Hicks—whatever do you mean?

DANTE

Tell me I don't have something to do with it.

CAITLIN

You don't have anything to do with it.

DANTE

You lie.

CAITLIN

Look how full of yourself you are.

DANTE

I just believe in giving credit where credit is due. And I believe that I'm the impetus behind your failure to wed.

CAITLIN

If I'm so nuts about you, then why am I having sex with an Asian design major?

DANTE
Jesus, you're caustic.

CAITLIN
I had to bring you down from that cloud you were floating on.
When I say I don't want to get married, I mean just that. I don't
want to marry anybody. Not for years.

DANTE
So who's asking? I don't want to marry you.

CAITLIN
Good. Stay in that frame of mind.

DANTE
But can we date?

CAITLIN
I'm sure Sang and—Veronica?—would like that.

DANTE
We could introduce them. They might hit it off.

CAITLIN
You're serious. You want to date again.

DANTE
I would like to be your boyfriend, yes.

CAITLIN
It's just the shock of seeing me after three years. Believe me,
you'll get over it.

DANTE
Give me a bit more credit. I think it's time we got back together,
you know. I'm more mature, you're more mature, you're finishing
college, I'm already in the job market . . .

CAITLIN
You work in a market, all right.

DANTE
Cute. Tell me you wouldn't want to go out again. After all the
talking we've been doing.

CAITLIN

The key word here is *talk,* Dante. I think the idea, the conception
of us dating is more idyllic than what actually happens when we
date.

DANTE

So . . . what? So we should just make pretend over the phone that
we're dating?

CAITLIN

I don't know. Maybe we should just see what happens.

DANTE

Let me take you out tonight.

CAITLIN

You mean, on a date?

DANTE

Yes. A real date. Dinner and a movie.

CAITLIN

The Dante Hicks Dinner and a Movie Date. I think I've been on
that one before.

DANTE

You have a better suggestion?

CAITLIN

How about the Caitlin Bree Walk on the Boardwalk, Then Get
Naked Somewhere Kind of Private Date?

DANTE

I hear that's a rather popular date.

CAITLIN
(hits him)
Jerk. Here I am, throwing myself at you, succumbing to your wily
charms, and you call me a slut, in so many words.

DANTE

What about Sing?

CAITLIN

Sang.

DANTE

Sang.

CAITLIN

He's not invited.

DANTE

He's your fiancé.

CAITLIN

I offer you my body and you offer me semantics? He's just a
boyfriend, Dante, and in case you haven't gotten the drift of why
I came all the way here from Ohio, I'm about to become single
again. And yes—let me placate your ego—you are the inspiration
for this bold and momentous decision, for which I'll probably be
ostracized at both school and home. You ask me who I choose, I
choose you.

DANTE

So what are you saying?

CAITLIN

You're such an asshole.

DANTE

I'm just kidding.

CAITLIN

I can already tell this isn't going to work.

DANTE

I'll ask Randal to close up for me—when he gets back.

CAITLIN

Where'd he go? I'd have thought he'd be at your side, like an
obedient lapdog.

DANTE

He went to rent a movie, but he hasn't gotten back yet. Ah, screw
it; I'll just lock the store up and leave him a note.

CAITLIN

You're too responsible. But no. I have to go home first. They don't even know I left school. And I should break the disengagement news to my mother, which is going to cause quite a row, considering she loves Sang.

DANTE

Who doesn't?

CAITLIN

Well, me I guess.
(gathering herself to go)
So, I shall take my leave of you, but I will return in a little while, at which time—yes—I would love to go for dinner and a movie with you.

DANTE

What happened to the walk and the nakedness?

CAITLIN

I'm easy, but I'm not that easy.
(she kisses his cheek)
See you later, handsome.

DANTE *watches her leave. He then explodes in jubilance.*

DANTE

YES!

Cut to:

INT: CONVENIENCE STORE. NIGHT

DANTE *looks ahead, dreamily, half-spinning in his chair.* RANDAL *enters carrying videos.*

RANDAL

Get to work.

DANTE
(takes videos)
What'd you rent?
(reads)
Best of Both Worlds?

RANDAL

Hermaphroditic porn. Starlets with both organs. You should see the box: Beautiful women with dicks that put mine to shame.

DANTE

And this is what you rented?

RANDAL

I like to expand my horizons.

DANTE

I got fined for selling cigarettes to a minor.

RANDAL

No way!

DANTE

Five hundred dollars.

RANDAL

You're bullshitting.

DANTE *hands him the summons.* RANDAL *reads it.*

RANDAL

I didn't think they even enforced this.

DANTE
(points to himself)

Living proof.

RANDAL

I thought you never sold cigarettes to kids.

DANTE

I don't; you did.

RANDAL
(pause)

Really?

DANTE

Little girl. Maybe five years old?

RANDAL
(taken aback)
Holy shit. That girl?

DANTE
As opposed to the hundreds of other children you let buy
cigarettes whenever you work here.

RANDAL
Then how come you got the fine?

DANTE
Because I'm here.

RANDAL
(incredulous)
You're lying.

DANTE
I swear. I couldn't make this kind of hell up.

RANDAL
Then why aren't you like screaming at me right now?

DANTE
Because I'm happy.

RANDAL
You're happy?

DANTE
I'm happy.

RANDAL
You're happy to get a fine?

DANTE
No, I'm happy because Caitlin came to see me.

RANDAL
Now I know you're lying.

DANTE
I'm not. She just left.

RANDAL

What did she say?

DANTE

She's not going to marry that guy. She went home to tell her mother.

RANDAL

You're kidding.

DANTE

I'm not.

RANDAL
(takes it in for a moment)
Wow. You've had quite an evening.

DANTE

She went home, she's getting ready, and we're going out.

RANDAL

I feel so ineffectual. Is there anything I can do for you?

DANTE

Watch the store while I go home and change.

RANDAL

What happened to title dictates behavior?

DANTE

This is my way of spitting water at life.

RANDAL
(suddenly aware)
Hey, what about Veronica?

DANTE

No! Don't bring it up. I don't want to think about that now. Let me enjoy this hour of bliss. I'll think about all of that later. In the meantime, nobody mentions the *V* word.

RANDAL

You're a snake.

DANTE

In my absence, try not to sell cigarettes to any newborns.

RANDAL

You want me to bring the VCR over here so we can watch this?

DANTE

I might be leaving early to go out with Caitlin, in which case you'll have to close the store tonight.

RANDAL

All right, but you're missing out. Chicks with dicks.

DANTE
(puts cat on counter)

I'll read the book.

DANTE *exits. A* CUSTOMER *comes back to the counter. He pets the cat.*

CUSTOMER

Cute cat. What's his name.

RANDAL

Peptic ulcer.

Cut to:

EXT: CONVENIENCE STORE. NIGHT

JAY *and* SILENT BOB *watch as* DANTE *passes. A small group of burners are poised around the store door.* JAY *carefully writes on a large piece of paper, using a thick marker.* SILENT BOB *hands him the scissors.* JAY *slowly cuts the large piece of paper.* SILENT BOB *hands him the tape.* JAY *snaps off a few pieces, and plasters the sign to the convenience store door. It is a large word balloon, and it reads* I EAT COCK! *Once in place, he raps on the window.* RANDAL *looks out, his face adjacent to the word balloon, making it appear as if he is saying he eats cock. The small group laughs hysterically. Cut to:*

INT: CONVENIENCE STORE. NIGHT

CAITLIN *enters, carrying an overnight bag.* RANDAL *is watching his porno. The porno is loud and lewd.* CAITLIN *stares.*

CAITLIN

Randal Graves—scourge of the video renter.

RANDAL

Ladies and gentlemen, Mrs. Asian Design Major herself: Caitlin Bree!

CAITLIN

You saw that article? God, isn't it awful? My mother sent that in.

RANDAL

I take it she likes the guy.

CAITLIN

You'd think she was marrying him. What are you watching?

RANDAL

Children's programming. What did your mom say when you told her you weren't engaged anymore?

CAITLIN

She said not to come home until graduation.

RANDAL

Wow, you got thrown out? For Dante?

CAITLIN

What can I say? He does weird things to me.

RANDAL

Can I watch?

CAITLIN

You can hold me down.

RANDAL

Can I join in?

CAITLIN

You might be let down. I'm not a hermaphrodite.

RANDAL

Few are. So what makes you think you can maintain a relationship with Dante this time around?

CAITLIN

A woman's intuition. Something in me says it's time to give the old boy a serious try.

RANDAL

Wow. Hey, I was just about to order some dinner. You eat Chinese, right?

CAITLIN

Dick.

RANDAL

Exactly.

CAITLAN

So where is he?

RANDAL

He went home to change for the big date.

CAITLIN

God, isn't he great?

RANDAL
(indicating TV)

No, *this* is great.

CAITLIN

Can I use the bathroom?

RANDAL

There's no light back there.

CAITLIN

Why aren't there any lights?

RANDAL

Well, there are, but for some reason they stop working at five-fourteen every night.

CAITLIN

You're kidding.

RANDAL

Nobody can figure it out. And the boss doesn't want to pay the electrician to fix it, because the electrician owes money to the video store.

CAITLIN

Such a sordid state of affairs.

RANDAL

And I'm caught in the middle—torn between my loyalty for the boss, and my desire to piss with the light on.

CAITLIN

I'll try to manage.

She heads toward the back.

RANDAL

Hey Caitlin . . .
                    (cautionary)
Break his heart again this time, and I'll kill you. Nothing personal.

CAITLIN

You're very protective of him, Randal. You always have been.

RANDAL

Territoriality. He was mine first.

CAITLIN
                    (rubs his head)
Awww. That was so cute.

She kisses his forehead and walks away. The MOTHER *and* SMALL
CHILD (Happy Scrappy) *come to the counter.*

MOTHER
                    (oblivious of the TV)
A pack of cigarettes.

The SMALL CHILD *points at the TV screen.*

SMALL CHILD

Cunt!

Cut to:

INT: CONVENIENCE STORE. NIGHT

RANDAL *studies the* I EAT COCK *word balloon.* DANTE *enters.*

DANTE

Who eats cock?

RANDAL

Bunch of savages in this town.
(recalling)
Hey, Caitlin's in the back. You might want to see if she's okay;
she's been back there a long time.

DANTE

There's no lights back there.

RANDAL

I told her that. She said she didn't need any. Why don't you join
her, man. Make a little bathroom bam-bam.

DANTE

I love your sexy talk. It's so . . . kindergarten: Poo-poo; wee-wee.

RANDAL

Fuck you.

The cooler door is heard opening. CAITLIN *walks lazily down the
convenience store aisle. She looks very satisfied.* DANTE *and* RANDAL
regard her curiously. She joins them, latching on to DANTE's *arm,
lovingly.*

CAITLIN

How'd you get here so fast?

DANTE

I left like an hour ago.

CAITLIN
(regards him curiously)
Do you always talk weird after you violate women?

RANDAL *and* DANTE *stare at* CAITLIN, *confused.*

RANDAL
Maybe the Asian design major slipped her some opium?

DANTE
Could be.

CAITLIN
(hugging DANTE)
Promise me it'll always be like that.

DANTE
Like what?

CAITLIN
When you just lie perfectly still and let me do everything.

DANTE
Um . . . okay.

RANDAL
Am I missing something here?

CAITLIN
I went back there, and Dante was already waiting for me.

RANDAL
He was?

CAITLIN
It was so cool. He didn't say a word. He was just . . . ready, you
know? And we didn't kiss or talk or anything. He just sat there
and let me do all the work.

RANDAL
(to DANTE)
You dog! I didn't see you go back there.

DANTE *is bewildered.*

CAITLIN

And the fact that there weren't any lights made it so . . .
(she lets out a growl and hugs DANTE)
God! That was so great!

DANTE
(quietly)
It wasn't me.

CAITLIN
(laughing it off)
Yeah, right. Who was it: Randal?

DANTE
(to RANDAL)
Was it you?

RANDAL

I was up here the whole time.

CAITLIN
(half-laughing)
You two better quit it.

DANTE

I'm serious.

CAITLIN
(beat)
We didn't just have sex in the bathroom?

DANTE

No.

Everyone is silent. Then . . .

CAITLIN

Stop this. This isn't funny.

DANTE

I'm not kidding. I just got back from outside.

CAITLIN
(covering her chest)
This isn't fucking funny, Dante!

DANTE
I'm not fooling around!
(to RANDAL)
Who went back there?

RANDAL
Nobody! I swear!

CAITLIN
I feel nauseous.

DANTE
Are you sure somebody was back there?

CAITLIN
(hits DANTE)
I didn't just fuck myself! Jesus, I'm going to be sick!

RANDAL
You just fucked a total stranger?

DANTE
Shut the fuck up!

CAITLIN
I can't believe this! I feel faint . . .

DANTE
(to RANDAL)
Call the police.

RANDAL
Why?

CAITLIN
No, don't!

DANTE
There's a strange man in our bathroom, and he just raped Caitlin!

                    CAITLIN
                    (weakly)
Oh God . . .

                    RANDAL
She said she did all the work.

                    DANTE
WOULD YOU SHUT THE FUCK UP?
                    (pause)
WHO THE FUCK IS IN THE BATHROOM?

Cut to:

INT: COVENIENCE STORE. LATER

THE OLD MAN'S FACE *is serene, almost happy, as he lies on a
stretcher. (Same* OLD MAN *who took a porn mag to the bathroom.)*

                    (OC) CORONER
Who is he?

The body bag zipper is pulled closed. DANTE, *the* CORONER, *and*
RANDAL *stand around the stretcher-bound body bag. The* CORONER
takes notes.

                    DANTE
I don't know. He just came in and asked to use the bathroom.

                    CORONER
What time was this?

                    DANTE
Um . . . I don't know
                    (to RANDAL)
What time did hockey end?

                    RANDAL
Around three or something.

                    DANTE
What time did we go to the funeral?

RANDAL

I think four.

CORONER

Wait a second? Who was working here today?

DANTE

Just me.

CORONER

I thought you just said you played hockey and went to a funeral.

DANTE

We did.

CORONER

Then who operated the store?

DANTE

Nobody. It was closed.

CORONER

With this guy locked in?

DANTE

Everything happened at once. I guess I forgot he was back there.

Ambulance attendants join them.

ATTENDANT 1

Can we take this now?

CORONER

Go ahead.

The stretcher is wheeled out. Midway down the body bag, something protrudes, pushing the bag up. It is an erection. RANDAL stares at it.

DANTE

Was he alive when . . . Caitlin . . .

CORONER

No. I place the time of death at about three-twenty.

RANDAL
Then how could she . . . you know . . .

CORONER
The body can maintain an erection after expiration. Sometimes
for hours. Did he have the adult magazine when he came in?

DANTE
No. I gave it to him.

RANDAL *and the* CORONER *stare in disbelief.*

DANTE
Well he asked me for it!

CORONER
(continuing)
I can't say for certain until we get him back to the lab, but my
guess is he was masturbating, his heart seized and he died. That's
when the girl found him.
(sniffing the air)
Something smells like shoe polish.

RANDAL
(to CORONER*)*
This has gotta be the weirdest thing you've ever been called in
on.

CORONER
(writing)
Actually, I once had to tag a kid that broke his neck trying to put
his mouth on his penis.

RANDAL *looks down, anonymously.*

DANTE
What about Caitlin?

CORONER
Shock trauma. She's going to need years of therapy after this. My
question is, How did she come to have sex with the dead man?

                              DANTE
         She thought it was me.

The CORONER *stares at* DANTE.

                             CORONER
         What kind of convenience store do you run here?

He exits. DANTE *and* RANDAL *stare at the floor.*

                             RANDAL
                              (beat)
         Do you think he was talking about my cousin?

Cut to:

EXT: VIDEO STORE. NIGHT

CAITLIN *sits in the back of the ambulance, a blanket draped over her
shoulders. An attendant takes her blood pressure. The doors are closed
and the vehicle speeds away.* JAY *and* SILENT BOB *lean against the
wall.* JAY *eats sugar out of a box.*

                               JAY
         I knew one of those motherfuckers was gonna kill somebody one
         day.

Cut to:

INT: CONVENIENCE STORE. NIGHT

*A jar of salsa is invaded by a large corn chip. Once in the condiment, the
corn chip resembles a surfacing shark fin. Fingers poke at it, bringing it
to life—swimming menacingly to and fro across the jar.*

                          (OC) RANDAL
                       (mumbling Jaws *theme)*
         Da-dum! Da-dum! Da-dum! DA-DUM! DA-DUM! DA-DUM!

DANTE *and* RANDAL *are on a freezer case.* RANDAL *pushes this chip
around the jar of salsa.* DANTE *stares up at the ceiling, oblivious.*

RANDAL

Salsa shark.

DANTE *says nothing.*

RANDAL
(as Brody)
"We're gonna need a bigger boat."

DANTE *says even less than nothing.*

RANDAL
(as Quint)
"Man goes into the cage; cage goes into the salsa; shark's in the salsa; our shark."

DANTE . . . *you know.*

RANDAL
(angry)
What? What's with you? You haven't said anything for like twenty minutes. What the hell is your problem?

DANTE
This life.

RANDAL
This life?

DANTE
Why do I have this life?

RANDAL
Have some chips; you'll feel better.

DANTE
I'm stuck in this pit, earning less than slave wages, working on my day off, dealing with every backward fuck on the planet, the goddam steel shutters are locked all day, I smell like shoe polish, I've got an ex-girlfriend who's catatonic after fucking a dead guy, and my present girlfriend has sucked thirty-six dicks.

RANDAL
Thirty-seven.

DANTE

My life is in the shitter right about now, so if you don't mind, I'd like to stew a bit.

(OC) CUSTOMER

You open?

RANDAL

Yeah.

RANDAL *hops off the freezer case and steps* OC.

(OC) RANDAL

That's all bullshit. You know what the real problem here is?

DANTE

I was born.

RANDAL *comes back.*

RANDAL

You should shit or get off the pot.

DANTE

I should shit or get off the pot.

RANDAL

Yeah, you should shit or get off the pot.

DANTE

What are you talking about?

RANDAL

I'm talking about this thing you have . . . this inability to improve your situation in life.

DANTE

Fuck you.

RANDAL

It's true. You'll sit there and blame life for dealing a cruddy hand, never once accepting the responsibility for the way your situation is.

DANTE

What responsibility?

RANDAL

All right, if you hate this job and the people, and the fact that you
have to come in on your day off, then quit.

DANTE

As if it's that easy.

RANDAL

It is. You just up and quit. There are other jobs, and they pay
better money. You're bound to be qualified for at least one of
them. So what's stopping you?

DANTE

Leave me alone.

RANDAL

You're comfortable. This is a life of convenience for you, and any
attempt to change it would shatter the pathetic microcosm you've
fashioned for yourself.

DANTE

Oh, like your life's any better?

RANDAL

I'm satisfied with my situation for now. You don't hear me
bitching. You, on the other hand, have been bitching all day.

DANTE

Thank you. Why don't you go back to the video store?

RANDAL

It's the same thing with Veronica.

DANTE

Leave her out of this.

RANDAL

You date Veronica because she's low maintenance and because
it's convenient. Meanwhile, all you ever do is talk about Caitlin.

You carry a torch for a girl you dated in high school—in high school for God's sake! You're twenty-two!

DANTE

Leave me alone.

RANDAL

If you want Caitlin, then face Veronica, tell her, and be with Caitlin. It you want Veronica, be with Veronica. But don't pine for one and fuck the other. Man, if you weren't such a fucking coward . . .

DANTE

. . . If I wasn't such a fucking coward.
(chuckles)
It must be so great to be able to simplify everything the way you do.

RANDAL

Am I right or what?

DANTE

You're wrong. Things happened today, okay? Things that probably ruined my chances with Caitlin.

RANDAL

What? The dead guy? She'll get over fucking the dead guy. Shit, my mom's been fucking a dead guy for thirty years; I call him Dad.

DANTE

Caitlin and I can't be together. It's impossible.

RANDAL

Melodrama coming from you seems about as natural as an oral bowel movement.

DANTE

What do you want me to say? Yes, I suppose some of the things you're saying may be true. But that's the way things are; it's not going to change.

RANDAL

Make them change.

DANTE

I can't, all right! Jesus, would you leave me alone? I can't make
changes like that in my life. If I could, I would—but I don't have
the ability to risk comfortable situations on the big money and the
fabulous prizes.

RANDAL

Who're you kidding? You can so.

DANTE

Jesus H. Christ, I can't!

RANDAL

So you'll continue being miserable all the time, just because you
don't have the guts to face change?

DANTE
(sadly)

My mother told me once that when I was three, my potty lid was
closed, and instead of lifting it, I chose to shit my pants.

RANDAL

Lovely story.

DANTE

Point is—I'm not the kind of person that disrupts things in order
to shit comfortably.

DANTE crosses OC. RANDAL appears contemplative. Cut to:

INT: CONVENIENCE STORE. NIGHT

DANTE repairs ripped dollar bills, taping them back together. JAY enters
with SILENT BOB and claps his hands.

JAY
(singing)

Noinch, noinch, noinch—smoking weed, smoking weed! Doing
coke! Drinking beers!
(to DANTE)
A pack of wraps, my good man. It's time to kick back, drink some
beers, and smoke some weed!

DANTE

Done poisoning the youth for the day?

JAY

Hell yes, whatever that means. Now I'm gonna head over to
Atlantic, drink some beers, get ripped, and—please God—get
laid.
(pulls out money)
E-Z Wider, one-and-a-halfs.

DANTE

One seventy-nine.

JAY
(to SILENT BOB)
Pay the good man.
(to DANTE)
Don't you close soon?

DANTE

A half hour.

JAY

We get off about the same time every night. We should hang out.
You get high?

DANTE

I should start.

JAY

Wanna come to this party tonight? There's gonna be some pussy
there, man!

DANTE

With you? I don't think so.

JAY

Listen to you. Oh shit. ''Oh, I don't hang out with drug dealers.''

DANTE

Nothing personal.

SILENT BOB *hands weed to* JAY.

JAY

I work, just like you. You're more of a crook than I am, dude.

DANTE

How do you figure . . . HEY! You can't roll a joint in here!

JAY
(rolling a joint)

Relax brother. What I mean is that you sell the stuff in this store
at the highest price around. A dollar seventy-nine for wraps—
what's that shit?

DANTE

It's not my store.

JAY

And these aren't my drugs—I just sell them.

DANTE

The difference is you exploit a weakness.

JAY

What's that mean?

DANTE

You sell to people that can't stay away from an addiction.

JAY

All right. How much is Pepsi here?

DANTE

A dollar sixty-nine, plus tax.

JAY

At Food City it's ninety-nine cents, plus tax.

DANTE

So.

JAY

So why do you sell it for so much more? I'll tell you
why—because people come here and they're like ''A dollar
eighty for soda? I should get it at Food City. But I don't feel like

driving there. I'll just buy it here so I don't have to drive up there.'' That's exploiting a weakness, too, isn't it?

DANTE

I can't believe you just rolled a joint in here.

JAY

Hey, man, what happened with that old guy?

DANTE

He died in the bathroom.

JAY

That's fucked up. Yo, I heard he was jerkin' off.

DANTE

I don't know. I wasn't watching.

JAY

Probably saw that Caitlin chick. I know I felt like beatin' it when I saw her.
(pantomimes sex)
Come here, bitch! You like this? Is this what you want? Hunhh?

DANTE

Knock it off. That used to be my girlfriend.

JAY

You used to go out with her?

DANTE

We were going to start again, I think.

JAY

Don't you already have a girlfriend?

DANTE

Veronica.

JAY

Is she that girl who's down here all the time? She came here today carrying a plate of food.

DANTE

Lasagne.

JAY

And what—you were gonna dump her to date that Caitlin chick?

DANTE

Maybe.

JAY

I don't know dude. That Caitlin chick's nice. But I see that Veronica girl doing shit for you all the time. She brings you food, she rubs your back . . . Didn't I see her change your tire one day?

DANTE

I jacked the car up. All she did was loosen the nuts and put the tire on.

JAY

Damn. She sure goes out of her way.

DANTE

She's my girlfriend.

JAY

I've had girlfriends, but all they wanted from me was weed and shit.

(beat)

Shit, my grandma used to say, "Which is better: a good plate with nothing on it . . ." No, wait. I fucked up. She said "What's a good-looking plate with nothing on it?"

DANTE

Meaning?

JAY

I don't know. She was senile and shit. Used to piss herself all the time. C'mon Silent Bob.

Exit JAY. SILENT BOB stands there.

SILENT BOB

You know, there's a million fine-looking women in the world, but they don't all bring you lasagne at work. Most of them just cheat on you.

SILENT BOB *leaves.* DANTE *shuts his eyes tightly and rubs the bridge of his nose with his thumb and forefinger, as if in deep concentration. He suddenly snaps his eyes open.*

                    DANTE
               (nearly surprised)
          He's right. I love her.

Cut to:

INT: VIDEO STORE. NIGHT

RANDAL *has a heart-to-heart with* VERONICA.

                    RANDAL
          So that's it. He doesn't love you anymore. He loves Caitlin.

VERONICA *stares, dumbfounded.*

                    VERONICA
          And . . . he told you all of this?

                    RANDAL
          Pretty much. All except the latent homosexuality part—that's just
          my theory.

                    VERONICA
          I . . . I don't know what to say.

                    RANDAL
          Don't hold it against him. He just never got Caitlin out of his
          system. It's not your fault. It's Dante.
               (beat)
          I don't know thing one about chicks. Do you want to cry or
          something? I can leave.

                    VERONICA
          I'm not sad.

                    RANDAL
          You're not?

VERONICA

No, I'm more furious. I'm pissed off. I feel like he's been killing
time while he tries to grow the balls to tell me how he really feels,
and then he can't even do it! He has his friend do it for him!

RANDAL

He didn't ask me to . . .

VERONICA

After all I've done for that fuck! And he wants to be with that
slut? Fine! He can have his slut!

RANDAL

Um, do you think you can give me a lift home tonight?

VERONICA
(oblivious of RANDAL)
I'm going to have a word with that asshole.

VERONICA storms out.

RANDAL

Wait! Veronica . . . I don't think . . .

RANDAL stares after her. A customer stands nearby.

RANDAL
(to customer)
What am I worried about? He'll probably be glad I started the
ball rolling. All he ever did was complain about her anyway. I'm
just looking out for his best interests. I mean, that's what a friend
does, am I right? I did him a favor.

CUSTOMER
(sees box on counter)
Oooh! Navy Seals!

Cut to:

INT: CONVENIENCE STORE. NIGHT

DANTE is on the ground holding his knee. VERONICA stands above him.

DANTE

What the fuck did you do that for?

VERONICA

If you didn't want to go out with me anymore, why didn't you just say it? Instead, you pussyfoot around and see that slut behind my back!

DANTE

What're you talking about?

VERONICA
(kicks him)
You've been talking to her on the phone for weeks!

DANTE

It was only a few times . . .

VERONICA

And then you pull that shit this morning, freaking out because I've gone down on a couple guys!

DANTE

A couple . . . ?

VERONICA
(throws purse at him)
I'm not the one trying to patch things up with my ex, sneaking around behind your back! And if you think that thirty-seven dicks are a lot, then just wait, mister: I'm going to put the hookers in Times Square to shame with all the guys I go down on now!

DANTE

Would you let me explain . . .

VERONICA

Explain what? How you were waiting until the time was right, and then you were going to dump me for her?

DANTE
(getting up)
Veronica . . . I . . . it's not like that anymore . . . I mean, it was never really like that . . .

VERONICA kicks him in the other leg. DANTE goes down, yelling in pain.

VERONICA
You're damn right it's not like that! Because I won't let it be like that! You want your slut? Fine! The slut is yours!

DANTE
I don't want Caitlin . . .

VERONICA
You don't know what you want, but I'm not going to sit here anymore holding your hand until you figure it out! I've encouraged you to get out of this fucking dump and go back to school, to take charge of your life and find direction. I even transferred so maybe you would be more inclined to go back to college if I was with you. Everyone said it was a stupid move, but I didn't care because I loved you and wanted to see you pull yourself out of this senseless funk you've been in since that whore dumped you, oh so many years ago. And now you want to go back to her so she can fuck you over some more?

DANTE
I don't want to go back with her . . .

VERONICA
Of course not; not now! You're caught, and now you're trying to snake out of doing what you wanted to do. Well, I won't let you. I want you to follow through on this, just so you can find out what a fucking idiot you are. And when she dumps you again—and she will, Dante, I promise you that—when she dumps you again, I want to laugh at you, right in your face, just so you realize that that was what you gave up our relationship for!
(grabs her purse)
I'm just glad Randal had the balls to tell me, since you couldn't.

DANTE
(weakly)
Randal . . . ?

VERONICA
And having him tell me . . . that was just the weakest move ever. You're spineless.

Veronica, I love you . . .

VERONICA

Fuck you.

VERONICA *exits.* DANTE *lies on the floor alone. Cut to:*

EXT: VIDEO STORE. NIGHT

RANDAL *exits and locks the door behind him. Cut to:*

INT: CONVENIENCE STORE. NIGHT

Tight on RANDAL'S *face as he steps inside.*

RANDAL

Dante?

Hands clasp around his throat and yank him out of the frame. DANTE
throttles RANDAL, *choking him to the ground.* RANDAL *throws his fists
into* DANTE'S *midriff, throwing him back into the magazine rack.*
RANDAL *jumps to his feet as* DANTE *comes at him again.* RANDAL
*tumbles into the cakes as Entenman's products scatter beneath and
around him. He grabs a pound cake and hits* DANTE *in the head with it,
using the opportunity to scurry down the middle aisle.* DANTE *leaps at
his feet, and* RANDAL *grabs the shelves, knocking aspirin over until*
RANDAL—*shrieking*—*sprays something in* DANTE'S *face.* DANTE
paws at his eyes. RANDAL *grabs Italian bread and smacks it into*
DANTE'S *face as he rushes him blindly.* DANTE *chases him out of the
frame. M&Ms scatter wildly across the empty floor, and the ruckus is
heard OC. Cut to:*

DANTE *and* RANDAL *later, out of breath, on the floor.* RANDAL *sits up
against the candy rack, rubbing his neck.* DANTE *lies on the floor, bacon
held against a sort of swelling eye. Both are pretty banged up. They are
surrounded by a mess of crushed cookies, ripped-open candies, broken
bread, and other damaged goods.*

RANDAL

How's your eye?

DANTE
(reluctantly)
The swelling's not so bad. But the FDS stings.
(beat)
How's your neck?

RANDAL
It's hard to swallow.

They are both silent. Then . . .

RANDAL
You didn't have to choke me.

DANTE
Why the fuck did you tell Veronica that I was going to dump her for Caitlin?

RANDAL
I thought I was doing you a favor.

DANTE
Thanks.

RANDAL

You were saying how you couldn't initiate change yourself, so I figured I'd help you out.

DANTE

Jesus.

Silence. Then . . .

RANDAL

You still didn't have to choke me.

DANTE

Oh please! I'm surprised I didn't kill you.

RANDAL

Why do you say that?

DANTE

Why do I say that? Randal . . . forget it.

RANDAL

No, really. What did I do that was so wrong?

DANTE

What don't you do? Randal, sometimes it seems like the only reason you come to work is to make my life miserable.

RANDAL

How do you figure?

DANTE

What time did you get to work today?

RANDAL

Like ten after.

DANTE

You were over half an hour late. Then all you do is come over here.

RANDAL

To talk to you.

DANTE

Which means the video store is ostensibly closed.

RANDAL

It's not like I'm miles away.

DANTE

Unless you're out renting videos at other video stores.

RANDAL

Hermaphrodites! I rented it so we could watch it together!

DANTE

You get me slapped with a fine, you fight with the customers and
I have to patch everything up. You get us chased out of a funeral
by violating a corpse. To top it all off, you ruin my relationship.
What's your encore? Do you anally rape my mother while
pouring sugar in my gas tank?
(sighs)
You know what the real tragedy is? I'm not even supposed to be
here today!

RANDAL
(suddenly outraged)
Fuck you. Fuck you, pal. Listen to you trying to pass the buck
again. I'm the source of all your misery. Who closed the store to
play hockey? Who closed the store to attend a wake? Who tried
to win back an ex-girlfriend without even discussing how he felt
with his present one? You wanna blame somebody, blame
yourself.
(beat, as DANTE)
"I'm not even supposed to be here today."
(whips stuff at DANTE)
You sound like an asshole. Whose choice was it to be here today?
Nobody twisted your arm. You're here today of your own volition,
my friend. But you'd like to believe that the weight of the world
rests on your shoulders—that the store would crumble if Dante
wasn't here. Well, I got news for you, jerk: This store would
survive without you. Without me either. All you do is
overcompensate for having what's basically a monkey's job: You
push fucking buttons. Any moron can waltz in here and do our
jobs, but you're obsessed with making it seem so much more
fucking important, so much more epic than it really is. You work

in a convenience store, Dante. And badly, I might add. And I
work in a shitty video store. Badly, as well.
                    (beat)
You know, that guy Jay's got it right—he has no delusions about
what he does. Us? We like to make ourselves seem so much better
than the people that come in here, just looking to pick up a paper
or—God forbid—cigarettes. We look down on them, as if we're
so advanced. Well, if we're so fucking advanced, then what are
we doing working here?

*RANDAL gets up, leaving DANTE to contemplate his strong words alone.
Cut to:*

DANTE and RANDAL silently clean up, backs to each other. Cut to:

DANTE places a mop in the corner. RANDAL pulls on his coat.

                    RANDAL
I threw out the stuff that got broken. The floor looks clean.

                    DANTE
You need a ride?

                    RANDAL
                (looks out door)
Got one. Just pulled up.

They stand in silence. Then . . .

                    DANTE
Do you work tomorrow?

                    RANDAL
Same time. What about you?

                    DANTE
I'm calling out. Going to hit the hospital—see how Caitlin is.
Then try to see Veronica.

                    RANDAL
You wanna grab something to eat tomorrow night . . . after I get
out of here?

DANTE
I'll call you. Let you know.

RANDAL
All right. Good luck with Veronica. If you want, I can talk to her,
you know, and explain . . .

DANTE
No thanks, I'll take care of it. We've got a lot of shit to talk about.

RANDAL
Helluva day.

DANTE
To say the least.

RANDAL
Do you need a hug or something? 'Cause I would have no hang-
ups about hugging you . . . you know, you being a guy and all.
Just don't knead my ass when you do it.

DANTE
Get the fuck outta here already.

RANDAL
I'm gone. I'll talk to you tomorrow.

RANDAL *exits. A second later, he reenters and tosses* DANTE *the sheet-
sign.*

RANDAL
You're closed.

He exits. DANTE *pushes the sign over from Open to Closed.*

DANTE *climbs behind the counter. He pops the register open and starts
counting the drawer out. The door is heard opening.*

POV JOHN: DANTE *counting out the register, not looking up.*

DANTE
What'd you forget something?
                    (looks up, surprised)
Oh. I'm sorry, we're closed.

A gunshot blasts out. DANTE flies back, his chest exploding. He stares ahead and slumps to the floor.

JOHN walks behind the counter, stepping over DANTE'S body on the floor, and takes the money out of the register. He grabs a paper bag and jams the money in it. He grabs handfuls of change, shoves it in his pocket, and then quickly exits the frame. DANTE continues to lie on the floor, unmoving.

CREDITS.

Credits end, and the door is heard opening. A customer comes to the counter and stands there. He waits, looks around for a clerk, looks down the aisles.

CUSTOMER

Hello? Little help?

No reply. He looks around again, and glances at the door to make sure nobody's coming in. Then he reaches behind the counter and grabs a pack of cigarettes. He leaves.

cast

Dante	**BRIAN O'HALLORAN**
Randal	**JEFF**
Veronica	**MARILYN GHIGLIOTTI**
Caitlin	**LISA SPOONAUER**
Jay	**JASON MEWES**
Silent Bob	**KEVIN SMITH**
Willam the Idiot Manchild	**SCOTT MOSIER**
Chewlies Rep	**SCOTT SCHIAFFO**
Old Man	**AL BERKOWITZ**
Woolen Cap Smoker	**WALT FLANAGAN**
Egg Man	**WALT FLANAGAN**
Offended Customer	**WALT FLANAGAN**
Cat-Admiring Bitter Customer	**WALT FLANAGAN**
Sanford	**ED HAPSTAK**
#812 Wynarski	**LEE BENDICK**
Hunting Cap Smoking Boy	**DAVID KLEIN**
Low-I.Q. Video Customer	
Hubcap Searching Customer	**DAVID KLEIN**
Coroner	**PATTI JEAN CSIK**
Administer of Fine	**KEN CLARK**
Indecisive Video Customer	**DONNA JEANE**
Caged Animal Masturbator	**VIRGINIA SMITH**

Dental School Video Customer	**BETSY BROUSSARD**
Trainer	**ERNEST O'DONNELL**
Alyssa's Sister Heather	**KIMBERLY LOUGHRAN**
Angry Hockey-Playing Customer	**SCOTT MOSIER**
Tabloid-Reading Customer	**GARY STERN**
Cat-Shit-Watching Customer	**JOE BAGNOLE**
Olaf the Russian Meathead	**JOHN HENRY WESTHEAD**
Stuck in Chips Can	**CHUCK BICKEL**
Jay's Lady Friend	**LESLIE HOPE**
"Happy Scrappy" Mom	**CONNIE O'CONNER**
Hockey Goalie	**VINCENT PERIERA**
Engagement Savvy Customer	**VINCENT PERIERA**
"Happy Scrappy" Kid	**ASHLEY PERIERA**
Bed-Wetting Dad/ Cold-Coffee Lover	**ERIX INFANTE**
Video Confusion/ Candy Confusion Customer	**MELISSA CRAWFORD**
Blue-Collar Man	**THOMAS BURKE**
Door-Tugging Customer	**DAN HAPSTAK**
Leaning Against Wall	**MITCH COHEN**
Burner Looking for Weed	**MATTHEW BANTA**
Cut-Off Customer	**RAJIV THAPER**
Orderly	**KEN CLARK**
Customer with Diapers	**MIKE BELICOSE**
Customer with Vaseline and Rubber Gloves	**JANE KURITZ**
MilkMaid	**GRACE SMITH**
Angry Mourners	**SCOTT MOSIER**
	ED HAPSTAK
	DAVE KLEIN
Little Smoking Girl	**FRANCES CRESCI**

Angry Crowd at Door	**MELISSA CRAWFORD**
	MATT CRAWFORD
	SARLA THAPAR
	LESLIE HOPE
	MITCH COHEN
	DAVID KLIEN
Hockey Players	**BRIAN DRINKWATER**
	BOB FISLER
	DEREK JACCODINE
Angry Smoking Crowd	**MATTHEW PERIERA**
	FRANK PERIERA
	CARL ROTH
	PAUL FINN
Dog	**HAIKU**
Cat	**LENIN'S TOMB**
Edit	**SCOTT MOSIER**
	KEVIN SMITH
Initial Incompetent Sound Editor	**SCOTT MOSIER**
Accomplished Sound Editor	**JAMES VON BUELOW**
Master Sound Mixer	**JAMES VON BUELOW**
Sync Fix	**JOIA SPECIALE**
Music	**BENJI GORDON**

"CLERKS"
Written by: S. Smyth and S. Angley
Performed by: Love Among Freaks

"KILL THE SEX PLAYER"
Written by: Girls Against Boys
Performed by: Girls Against Boys
Courtesy of Touch and Go Records

"GOT ME WRONG"
Written by: J. Cantrell
Performed by: Alice In Chains
Courtesy of Columbia Records

"MAKING ME SICK"
Written by: T. Stinson, G. Gershunoff, R. Bradbury
Performed by: Bash and Pop
Courtesy of Sire Records by arrangement with Warner Special Products

"CHEWBACCA"
Written by: Art, Hank, Dave
Performed by Supernova

"GO YOUR OWN WAY"
Written by: Lindsey Buckingham
Performed by: Seaweed
Courtesy of Sub Pop Records

"PANIC IN CICRO"
Written by: The Jesus Lizard
Performed by: The Jesus Lizard
Courtesy of Touch and Go Records

"SHOOTING STAR"
Written by: Paul Rodgers
Performed by: Golden Smog
Courtesy of Crackpot Records

"LEADERS AND FOLLOWERS"
Written by: G. Graffin
Performed by: Bad Religion
Courtesy of Atlantic Recording Corp., and Sony Music, a group of Sony Music
Entertainment, Inc.

"VIOLENT MOOD SWINGS" (Thread Mix)
Written by: W. Fickus, C. Hall, J. Sellers, D. Suycott, S. Zuchman
Performed by: Stabbing Westward
Courtesy of Columbia Records

"BERSERKER"
Written by: S. Smyth, S. Angley and K. Smith
Performed by Love Among Freaks

"BIG PROBLEMS"
Written by: R. Mullen and W. Weatherman
Performed by: Corrosion of Conformity
Courtesy of Sony Music

"CAN'T EVEN TELL" (Theme from *Clerks*)
Written by: D. Pirnet
Performed by: Soul Asylum
Courtesy of Columbia Records

Soundtrack Available on Chaos/Columbia Records

Postproduction Supervisor
CHARLIE McLELLAN

Camera Operator	**DAVID KLEIN**
Lighting Assistant	**ED HAPSTAK**
Occasional Camera Assistant	**VINCENT PERIERA**
Occasional Grips	**VINCENT PERIERA**
	RAJIV THAPAR
Gaffer	**ED HAPSTAK**
Trouble Shooter	**ED HAPSTAK**
Sound Mixer	**SCOTT MOSIER**
Boom	**WHOEVER GRABBED THE POLE**
Makeup	**LESLIE HOPE**
Cat Wrangler	**VINCENT PERIERA**
Occasional Continuity	**TARA DAUST**
Production Stills	**ED HAPSTAK**
Catering	**QUICK STOP CONVENIENCE**
Cameras by	**PRO CAMERA AND LIGHTING**
Sound Mixed at	**SOUND HOUND**

Title by	**REI MEDIA GROUP**
Postproduction Equipment by	**SPERA GROUP**
Legal Eagle	**JOHN SLOSS**
Czar of Representation	**JOHN PIERSON**

thanks

Quick Stop Convenience

R.S.T. Video

Jan Film Lab

Steve and Choice Video

Postens Funeral Parlor

First Avenue Playhouse

Film Video Arts

Bubba Shea

Mr. and Mrs. Hapstak

Traci Lapanne

Leonardo First Aid

Kenneth Schneider

John and Carol Mosier

Butch and Mary Lou King

Tim Hill and the Borough of Highlands

The New School for Social Research

Henry Hudson Regional

The Doonsbury Company

D.C. Comics

Maysle's

Sound One

Magno

The Residents of Leonardo

Amy Taubin

Peter Broderick

David Linde

Larry Kardish

Geoff Gilmore

Janet Pierson

the director would like to thank

God—For the gifts
Mom and Dad—For all the support
Scott—For accepting an invitation to lunch
Walt—For a copy of "Dark Knight Returns"
Ed—For being a Magpie
Kim—For seven years
Kristin—For patience, perseverance and love
Vincent—For the inspiration
Dave—For all the pretty pictures
Jason—For being Jason
Bry—For taking nothing seriously
Virginia—For saying "Be a filmmaker"
Brother Don—For always picking up the check
Toni and Landmark—For all the possibilities
Mr. and Mrs. Thapar—For being as understanding as parents
Ann and Andy—For the cash
Karen Lapointe—For the note
Larry Baroujian—For not turning me in
John "My Hero" Pierson—For having second thoughts
Bob Hawk—For having nothing better to do on 10/3/93
Mark "Doctor Love" Tusk—For not giving up
Harvey Weinstein—For an unforgettable order of potato skins
and
Hal Hartley, Richard Linklater
Spike Lee and Jim Jarmusch—For leading the way.